A JUMPIN' JIM'S UKULELE SONGBOK

The DAILY UKULELE

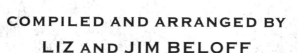

LEAP YEAR EDITION
366 More Great Songs For Better Living

COMPILED AND ARRANGED BY

LIZ AND JIM BELOFF

Copyright @ 2012 FLEA MARKET MUSIC, INC.

HAL•LEONARD®
CORPORATION
7777 W. BLUEMOUND RD. P.O. BOX 13819 MILWAUKEE, WI 53213

Edited by Ronny S. Schiff
Cover and Art Direction by Elizabeth Maihock Beloff
Graphics and Music Typography by Charylu Roberts
Illustrations by Pete McDonnell

Contents

Foreword

Encore! After hearing about the joy that individual players and ukulele clubs have had in strumming and singing through *The Daily Ukulele* songbook, we were inspired to see if we could put together another large collection of songs. Since 2012 is a leap year, we used that as a reason to find an additional 366 "great songs for better living," and now here it is: *The Daily Ukulele: Leap Year Edition*!

In combing through thousands of possible entries for this book, we once again sought out well-known songs that were relatively easy to play and sing and appropriate for one person or a hundred to perform. Another key consideration was whether a particular song adapted well to four strings. While there are few popular songs that haven't been attempted on a ukulele, some seem to be especially "strum-worthy." It's no surprise then, that the majority of songs in this book have strong melodies and great chord changes. Many of the best-loved standards, movie themes, musical theater showstoppers and pop hits from the '50s, '60s, '70s right up to today continue to resonate because of their durable tunes and clever chording.

Any songbook reflects the personal tastes of the compilers and this one certainly includes many of our favorite songs and songwriters. At the same time, we benefited from hundreds of song suggestions that were sent to us from other players who have developed their own feelings about what makes a great ukulele song. We are grateful for all of those suggestions and happy to report that many are included here.

More than a few people have commented that *The Daily Ukulele* taught them how to play. Although that wasn't the original intent, it makes sense that if a book is filled with songs you want to learn, it can act as a great inspiration. We are confident that this book is full of many more great songs you'll want to learn, and will play an ongoing role in improving your technique. More than that, though, we hope this book brings you the unique pleasure that comes from making music, either on your own or with others, for years to come. Especially on a leap year!

Keep on strummin',

Liz and Jim Beloff
Clinton, Connecticut
2012

www.fleamarketmusic.com
www.thedailyukulele.com

Song Index

Ukulele 101

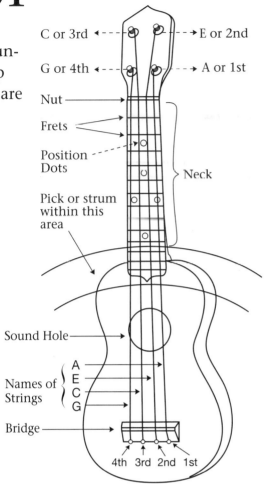

The songs in this book are arranged for ukuleles in C tuning. In this tuning, the individual strings from the top (closest to your nose) to bottom (closest to your toes) are tuned GCEA.

Uke C Tuning

One easy way to tune a ukulele is with a pitchpipe or electronic tuner matching the strings with the notes.

This corresponds to that famous melody:

Here are the notes on the piano:

Keeping In Tune

Most ukuleles have friction tuners that include a small screw at the end of the tuner. The secret to staying in tune is to keep these screws tight enough so that the tuners don't slip, but loose enough that the tuners still turn.

Holding The Uke

Press your uke against your body about two-thirds of the way up your forearm. Your strumming hand should naturally fall on top of the upper frets (not over the soundhole). Hold the neck of the uke between your thumb and first finger of your other hand, so that your fingers are free to move about the fretboard.

Note: See *Jumpin' Jim's Ukulele Tips 'N' Tunes* if you need a basic ukulele method book.

Making The Chords

You make chords by putting various combinations of fingers on the fretboard. In this songbook, you'll find chord diagrams that show where to put your fingers to make the right sound. The vertical lines in the diagrams represent strings and the horizontal lines represent the frets. The numbers at the bottom of the chords shown below indicate what fingers to use.

1 = Index finger
2 = Second finger
3 = Ring finger
4 = Pinky

C Chord

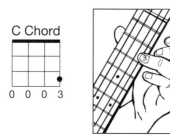

0 0 0 3

F Chord

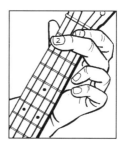 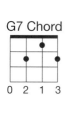

2 0 1 0

G7 Chord

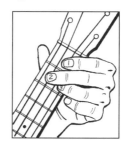

0 2 1 3

Remember to:

1. When pressing down the strings, use the tips of your fingers.
2. Always press down in the space between the frets, not on them.
3. Press the strings down to the fretboard. If you hear a buzz it may be because you are not pressing hard enough or are too close to a fret.
4. Keep your thumb at the back of the neck, parallel to the frets.

Making The Strums

The Common Strum: This is the most basic up/down strum. It can be produced solely with your index finger going down the strings with the fingernail and up with the cushion of your fingertip. You can also try this with the pad of your thumb running down the strings and the tip of your index finger going up. This strum will work fine on many of the songs in this book. Two good examples would be "April Showers" and "Tip-Toe Thru' The Tulips With Me."

Waltz Strum: This 3/4 rhythm can be produced simply with your thumb or index finger in sets of three down strums. You can use this on 3/4 songs like "Morning Has Broken" and "Somewhere My Love."

Island Strum: This lilting, syncopated strum is a combination of quick up and down strums plus a roll. In a typical 4-beat measure it would look like this:

⊓ = downstroke

∨ = upstroke

⊓   *roll* ∨   ∨   ⊓ ∨

Here's how to make the roll strum.

One and **Two** and **Three** and **Four** and…

Play the downstroke with your thumb and the upstroke with your index finger. The roll is made by running the ring, middle and index fingers quickly in succession across the strings. You can also substitute a downstroke for the roll if that is easier. Variations of this handy strum can be used on songs like "Anticipation," "The Banana Boat Song," "Black Magic Woman" and countless others in the book.

Tremolo: This is used often as an ending flourish for a song. It's produced by running your index finger across the strings rapidly. Try this at the end of any song where you want a "big finish."

How To Use This Book

The best way to use this songbook is, well, daily. Because there are 366 songs you can play a different song each day for a whole year, including leap day (February 29th)! The songs are not in strict alphabetical order, so consult the index in front when in doubt.

Many of the songs included here should be easy for you to play and sing right away. Here are a few things to note that will make this songbook especially enjoyable:

1. **Chord Grids:** Just in case you need a reminder of how to make a certain chord, the chord grids for each song are directly under the title, in order of their appearance. The *Chord Chart* on page 12 shows suggested fingerings.

2. **First Note:** This shows the first singing note of the song. Keep in mind that the lowest note on a GCEA-tuned "my dog has fleas" uke is middle C. As a result, when the first note of a song is below middle C (for example the B in "Ain't No Sunshine") the note shown is actually an octave above. Play that note and then sing the octave below.

3. **N.C.** Whenever you see N.C. above the staff that means "no chord," a place in the song where you should stop playing until you get to the next chord. This "break" can be a nice flourish that will add drama to your performance. Two good examples of this are in "No Particular Place To Go" and "A Teenager In Love."

4. **Chords in Parentheses:** These alternate chords should be played during the last time on those measures. When the chord in parentheses is placed very close to another chord it should replace the chord to the left. Otherwise it is in addition to the other chords in the measure. An example of this is in "Old Cape Cod." For the second ending, play the E7, A7, D and D7 chords across those three measures. For the third ending (and end of the song) play E7, A7, D, Em7 and D. Do not play the D7.

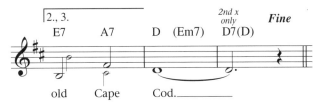

There are some additional symbols that you'll see used throughout the arrangements in this songbook.

Repeat Signs: Play the section within the signs again before going on to the next section.

First Ending: Play through the measures under this bracketed area and then go back to the beginning of that section. Then look for further endings.

D.C.   **Da Capo:** This means "from the beginning." Go back to the beginning of the music.

D.S.   **Dal Segno:** Means to look for the 𝄋 sign and repeat that section from the sign.

Coda: Ending section. When you see "*To Coda* ⊕" jump ahead to the closing section that begins with this symbol

Cue Notes: These smaller notes (and rests) in the measures correspond with the lyrics below the top verse.

The Arrangements

Over the years of publishing our Jumpin' Jim's songbooks we've fine-tuned our approach to arranging songs for the ukulele. Often it's a careful balancing act between finding a uke-friendly playing key while also keeping the melody in a comfortable singing range. The most uke-friendly playing keys for ukuleles in C tuning (GCEA) are C, F, G, D and A, with C and G being the easiest. For a mixed audience of male and female voices of all ages, we try to keep the melodies between G below middle C and C above middle C. With this songbook, we also kept in mind comfortable singing keys for women on songs especially associated with female artists. Examples of this include Lulu's "To Sir With Love" and Cyndi Lauper's "Time After Time." Both of those songs are either in the original keys or very close to them. As a result, the melody in most of the songs in this book will include single notes that are too low to be picked on a re-entrant, high G, "my dog has fleas" ukulele. For those who want to pick those lower notes, a C-tuned uke with a lowered G string will do the trick.

Transposing

Hopefully, most of the songs in this book are in keys that are easy for you to play and sing. In case a particular song feels too high or too low, you have the option of transposing it to a more comfortable key. If the song is in G and it feels a little high, try dropping the song one whole step down to F. That should be fairly easy to do, since every chord in the arrangement comes down one whole step. G drops to F, C drops to B♭ and D7 drops to C7 and so on. If the song is in F and feels a bit low try going up to G and raising the chords a whole step. With a bit of experience, you should be able to do this in real time, as you are playing the song in tempo. The same would apply for transposing songs from A to G and D to C. If the song still feels too high or low, you may want to try a more dramatic transposition, like G to C or F to C and vice versa.

With some experience, you'll become very familiar with the chords that typically appear in uke-friendly keys and will be transposing easily and quickly from one key to the next. This is especially true for simpler songs with a minimum of chords like blues and folk tunes. The transposition chart below will help you keep track of the essential chords in the most uke-friendly keys:

Chords in	C	C	F	G7	Am	Dm	E7
	D	D	G	A7	Bm	Em	F♯7
	F	F	B♭	C7	Dm	Gm	A7
	G	G	C	D7	Em	Am	B7
	A	A	D	E7	F♯m	Bm	C♯7

For example, if you wish to transpose a song in the key of C to the key of D, you would

	The Original Chord		**The New Chord**
Change	C	to	D
Change	F	to	G
Change	G7	to	A7
Change	Am	to	Bm
Change	Dm	to	Em
Change	E7	to	F♯7

In this case, everything moves up one whole step.

Notes On Some Of The Songs

by Jim Beloff

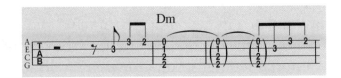

And I Love Her: There are a number of songs in the book that feature well-known instrumental licks. In several of them, I turned those licks into ukulele tablature and highlighted it as a special grayed-out section. Uke tablature is a very simple way of showing what frets and strings to play to make the correct notes. The strings of the uke are represented by four lines starting with G on the bottom and going up to C, E and A. The number on the strings refers to the correct fret to play. In this song, the first measure of the uke tab section tells you to play the third fret of the E string and then the third fret of the A string, followed by the second fret of the same string. The next measure represents a Dm chord in uke tab. With these sections, you always have the option of simply strumming the chords above the tablature. If playing with others, have some of them play the notes while others strum the chords.

Bang The Drum All Day: Since the early 1970s, I have been a major Todd Rundgren fan and have always dreamed of including his songs in our songbooks. That's why I'm thrilled that we are able to include "I Saw The Light" and "Bang The Drum All Day" in this collection. Because Todd has been known to play "Bang The Drum…" on a ukulele in concert, I contacted him to see if he would be willing to contribute an additional verse that referenced the ukulele. Thank you, Todd for the special extra lyric!

Call Me: This song is one of many in the book that uses an Fmaj7 chord, one of the more challenging chords to make on a ukulele. You start with a simple F chord, but then you have to extend your ring finger to the third fret of the A string and stretch your pinky out to the fourth fret of the C string. For inexperienced players, making this chord can slow down the flow of a song. There is a much easier second position alternative, which is made by playing the fifth frets of both the G and C strings. While that inversion sounds fine here, it can sometimes sound a bit out of context with other first position chords. A last resort is to play an F chord in place of any Fmaj7. This may sound okay in certain situations (especially for brief moments) but be aware that the major seventh chord has a unique sound that can't be replaced by a simple major chord. The good news is that the more you play the first position version the easier it is to make!

Fmaj7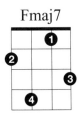

Fmaj7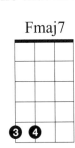

F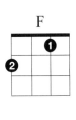

Can't Smile Without You: The multiple key changes here are a big part of why this song became such a major hit for Barry Manilow. They also make it a lot of fun to play and sing!

Candy: The chord changes on this song seem to fall into each other. Smooth just like the song itself.

Circle Of Life: I've always been hypersensitive to unexpected chord changes. The first time I heard this song I was immediately struck by Elton John's unique chord change in the chorus after the lyric, "on the path un-winding." The melody and chords that lead up to it build the tension, so that when we finally hear the E♭(add2) it acts as an unexpected but satisfying release. I'm also delighted at how satisfying this series of chords sounds on four strings.

Homeward Bound: All of the songs in this book can be strummed in one way or another. Some, like this song, can really shine with a simple picking pattern. This one below will work for "Homeward Bound" and many of the other folk songs in the book.

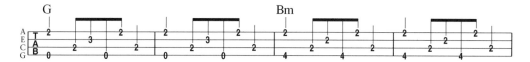

I'll Never Fall In Love Again: Burt Bacharach songs seem to sound especially great on the ukulele. His melodies and chord changes are always interesting and often include major seven chords. Like "Call Me" this song includes an Fmaj7. The "stretch" first position version sounds best, but you can always substitute the second position version (see "Call Me") or, if necessary, an F major chord.

I'll See You In My Dreams: There are a few ways to fret the Fm6 chord in this song. The most obvious is to place your index finger across all the strings at the first fret and then use your middle finger to press the second fret of the C string and ring finger to press the third fret of the A string. You can also think of it like a four-fingered diminished chord with the pinky moving up one fret. If it's still too difficult, you can always fret a G7sus chord, but you'll need to avoid playing the G string. In this case, you'll only strum the highest 3 strings.

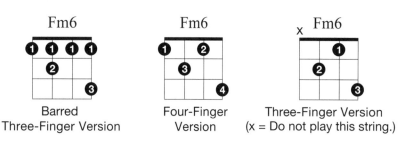

It's A Sin To Tell A Lie: This song was originally written in ¾ time as reflected in the arrangement here, but it can just as easily work in 4/4 with the same chords.

Lazy Day: While I have always enjoyed the original recording by Spanky And Our Gang, I had no idea how chordally complex it is. There are 23 different chords here, although none of them are very difficult to make. The melody has a roller-coaster quality to it, twisting this way and that and at every turn an interesting chord. It's a lot of fun!

Leap For A Man, Girls, It's Leap Year: I discovered the sheet music for this at a local flea market. How could we resist?

Love Is In The Air: In 2009 Liz and I toured Australia, performing and giving workshops across the country. In Melbourne we performed with the Melbourne Ukulele Kollective or MUK. I'll never forget their enthusiastic performance of this disco hit by Australian pop singer, John Paul Young.

Ram On: This was a short song on Ram, Paul McCartney's second solo album. He played it on a ukulele.

A Ukulele And You: A quote by Bette Midler was the inspiration for this song of mine. In an interview she said, "...I'm also learning the ukulele. And if push comes to shove, I will be out there with that ukulele all by myself..."

Ukulele Central: Chris Leslie and Ric Sanders, two members of the English folk-rock group Fairport Convention, wrote this song. As to its creation, Chris Leslie writes, "I was over at Ric's place one afternoon when he played me something he had just written on the uke. He wondered if I might come up with some words for it. I had just finished reading *The Ukulele: A Visual History* by Jim Beloff. The words just flew out that night. We had the song finished next morning. It has become part of Fairport Convention's shows...on five ukes!"

White Sandy Beach: A beautiful song made famous by Israel Kamakawiwo'ole. Enjoy!

Chord Chart

Major Chords

A, A♯/B♭, B, C, C♯/D♭, D, D♯/E♭, E, F, F♯/G♭, G, G♯/A♭

Minor Chords

Am, A♯m/B♭m, Bm, Cm, C♯m/D♭m, Dm, D♯m/E♭m, Em, Fm, F♯m/G♭m, Gm, G♯m/A♭m

Dominant Seventh Chords

A7, A♯7/B♭7, B7, C7, C♯7/D♭7, D7, D♯7/E♭7, E7, F7, F♯7/G♭7, G7, G♯7/A♭7

Minor Seventh Chords

Am7, A♯m7/B♭m7, Bm7, Cm7, C♯m7/D♭m7, Dm7, D♯m7/E♭m7, Em7, Fm7, F♯m7/G♭m7, Gm7, G♯m7/A♭m7

Major Sixth Chords

A6, A♯6/B♭6, B6, C6, C♯6/D♭6, D6, D♯6/E♭6, E6, F6, F♯6/G♭6, G6, G♯6/A♭6

Minor Sixth Chords

Am6, A♯m6/B♭m6, Bm6, Cm6, C♯m6/D♭m6, Dm6, D♯m6/E♭m6, Em6, Fm6, F♯m6/G♭m6, Gm6, G♯m6/A♭m6

Major Seventh Chords

Amaj7, A♯maj7/B♭maj7, Bmaj7, Cmaj7, C♯maj7/D♭maj7, Dmaj7, D♯maj7/E♭maj7, Emaj7, Fmaj7, F♯maj7/G♭maj7, Gmaj7, G♯maj7/A♭maj7

Augmented Fifth Chords (+ or aug)

A+, A♯+/B♭+, B+, C+, C♯+/D♭+, D+, D♯+/E♭+, E+, F+, F♯+/G♭+, G+, G♯+/A♭+

Diminished Seventh Chords (dim)

Adim, A♯dim/B♭dim, Bdim, Cdim, C♯dim/D♭dim, Ddim, D♯dim/E♭dim, Edim, Fdim, F♯dim/G♭dim, Gdim, G♯dim/A♭dim

"A"–You're Adorable
(The Alphabet Song)

Words and Music by BUDDY KAYE,
SIDNEY LIPPMAN and FRED WISE

Ac-Cent-Tchu-Ate The Positive

Words by
JOHNNY MERCER

Music by
HAROLD ARLEN

Act Naturally

Words and Music by VONIE MORRISON
and JOHNNY RUSSELL

Ain't No Sunshine

Words and Music by
BILL WITHERS

I know, I know, I know,__ I know, I know, I know, hey,__ I ought to leave the young thing a - lone,__

D.C. al Coda

Em7   Bm7   D

__ but ain't no sun - shine when she's__ gone, whoa,__ whoa, whoa,__ whoa.

Coda

Em7   Repeat 3 times   Bm7   D   Em7(add9)

An - y - time__   she goes a - way.

Allegheny Moon

Words and Music by
DICK MANNING
and AL HOFFMAN

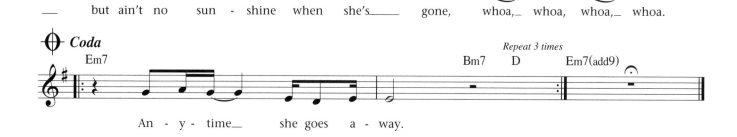

FIRST NOTE

Slowly

D

Al - le - ghe - ny moon, I need your light to help me find ro - mance to -

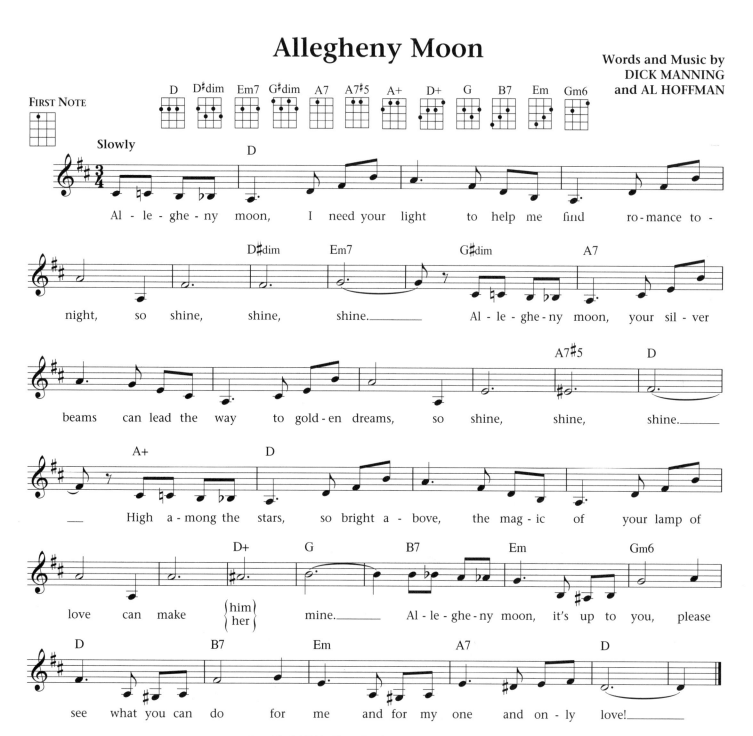

D#dim   Em7   G#dim   A7

night, so shine, shine, shine._____ Al - le - ghe - ny moon, your sil - ver

A7#5   D

beams can lead the way to gold - en dreams, so shine, shine, shine._____

A+   D

__ High a - mong the stars, so bright a - bove, the mag - ic of your lamp of

D+   G   B7   Em   Gm6

love can make {him/her} mine._____ Al - le - ghe - ny moon, it's up to you, please

D   B7   Em   A7   D

see what you can do for me and for my one and on - ly love!

Alabamy Bound

**Words by B.G. DeSYLVA
and BUD GREEN**

**Music by
RAY HENDERSON**

I'm Al - a - bam - y bound;_____ there'll be no "hee - bie jee - bies" hang - in' 'round._____ Just gave the mean - est tick - et man on earth,___ all I'm worth___ to put my toot - sies in an up - per berth.___

Just hear that choo - choo sound;_____ I know that soon we're goin' to
I'm just a luck - y hound_____ to have some - one to put my

cov - er ground._____ And then I'll hol - ler so the world will know,___
arms a - round._____ That's why I'm shout - in' for the world to know,___

"Here I go,"___ I'm Al - a - bam - y bound. I'm Al - a - bound.___

All The Way

Words by
SAMMY CAHN

Music by
JAMES VAN HEUSEN

Amapola
(Pretty Little Poppy)

New English Words by
ALBERT GAMSE

By JOSEPH M. LACALLE

April Showers

Words by
B.G. DeSYLVA

Music by
LOUIS SILVERS

Though A - pril show - ers may come your way, they bring the flow - ers that bloom in May; so if it's rain - ing,___ have no re - grets___ — be - cause it is - n't rain - ing rain you know, it's rain - ing vi - o - lets. And where you see clouds up - on the hills, you soon will see crowds of daf - fo - dils; so keep on look - ing for a blue - bird and lis - t'ning for his song, when - ev - er A - pril show - ers come a - long.

Anticipation

Words and Music by
CARLY SIMON

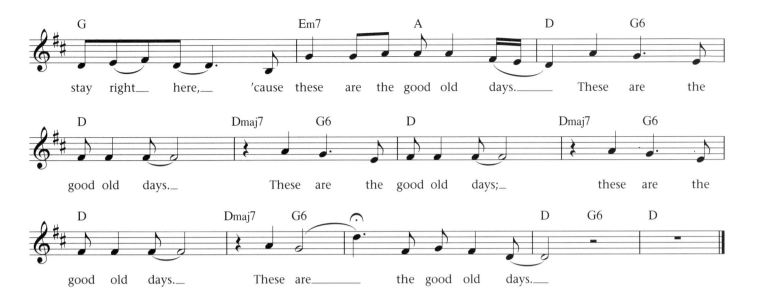

stay right here, 'cause these are the good old days. These are the
good old days. These are the good old days; these are the
good old days. These are the good old days.

Annie's Song

Words and Music by
JOHN DENVER

1., 3. You fill up my sens - es like a night in a for - est,
2. Come let me love you, let me give my life to you,

like the moun - tains in spring - time, like a walk in the
let me drown in your laugh - ter, let me die in your

rain. Like a storm in the des - ert, like a
arms. Let me lay down be - side you, let me

sleep - y blue o - cean, you fill up my sens -
al - ways be with you. Come let me love

es, come fill me a - gain.
you, come love me a - gain.

And I Love Her

Words and Music by JOHN LENNON and PAUL McCARTNEY

As Tears Go By

Words and Music by MICK JAGGER, KEITH RICHARDS and ANDREW LOOG OLDHAM

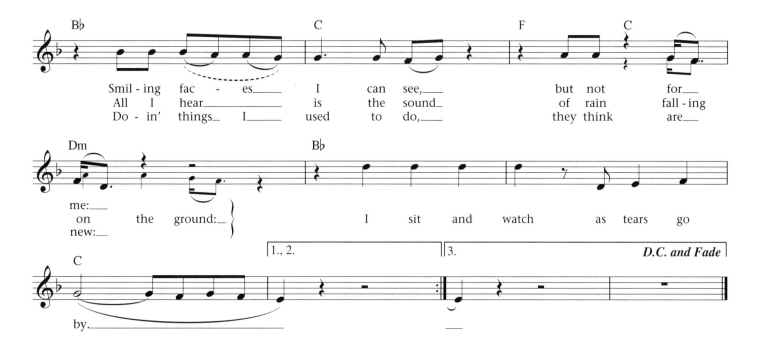

Smil - ing fac - es___ I can see,___ but not for___
All I hear___ is the sound___ of rain fall - ing
Do - in' things___ I___ used to do,___ they think are___

me:___ on the ground:___ } I sit and watch as tears go
new:___

1., 2.   3.   *D.C. and Fade*

by.___

Atlantis

**Words and Music by
DONOVAN LEITCH**

C   D   F   G

Moderately

C   D   F

Spoken: The continent of Atlantis was an island which lay before the great flood in the area we now call the Atlanic Ocean.
Kings colonized the world. All the gods who play in the mythological dramas in all legends from all lands were from fair Atlantis.

C   G   C   D

So great an area of land, that from her western shores, those beautiful sailors journeyed to the South and the North Americas with ease, in their
Knowing her fate, Atlantis sent out ships to all corners of the earth. On board were the twelve, the poet,

F   C   G   C

ships with painted sails.   To the east, Africa was a neighbor across
the physician, the farmer, the scientist, the magician, and the other so-called gods of our legends. Tho' gods they were and as the elders of our time

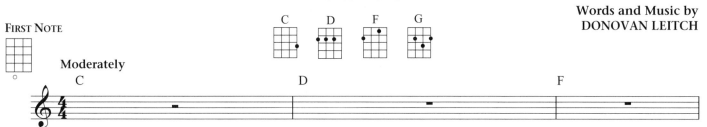

D   F   1.   2.
                                C   G   C   G

a short strait of sea miles. The great Egyptian age is but a remnant of the Atlantian culture. The antedeluvian
choose to remain blind, let us rejoice and let us sing and dance and ring   in the new. Hail Atlantis! Way

Repeat and Fade

C   D   F   C   G

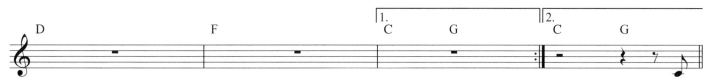

down___ be - low___ the o - cean___ where___ I wan - na be,___ she may be,___ Way___

Copyright © 1968 by Donovan (Music) Ltd.
Copyright Renewed
All Rights Administered by Peer International Corporation

25

Are You Havin' Any Fun?

Words by
JACK YELLEN

Music by
SAMMY FAIN

As Time Goes By

Words and Music by
HERMAN HUPFELD

Autumn Leaves

English Lyric by
JOHNNY MERCER

French Lyric by
JACQUES PREVERT

Music by
JOSEPH KOSMA

Back In The Saddle Again

Words and Music by
GENE AUTRY and RAY WHITLEY

1. I'm back in the sad-dle a-gain; out where a
2. Rid-in' the range once more; tot-in' my

friend is a friend. Where the long-horn cat-tle feed on the
old for-ty - four. Where you sleep out ev-'ry night; where the

1.
low-ly jim-son weed, I'm back in the sad-dle a-gain.
on-ly law is right, I'm

2.
back in the sad-dle a-gain. Whoo-pi - ti - yi - yo,

rock-in' to and fro, back in the sad-dle a-gain. Whoo-pi - ti - yi -

yay, I go my way, back in the sad-dle a-gain.

The Banana Boat Song

Lyric and Music by ERIK DARLING,
BOB CAREY and ALAN ARKIN

Bang The Drum All Day

Words and Music by
TODD RUNDGREN

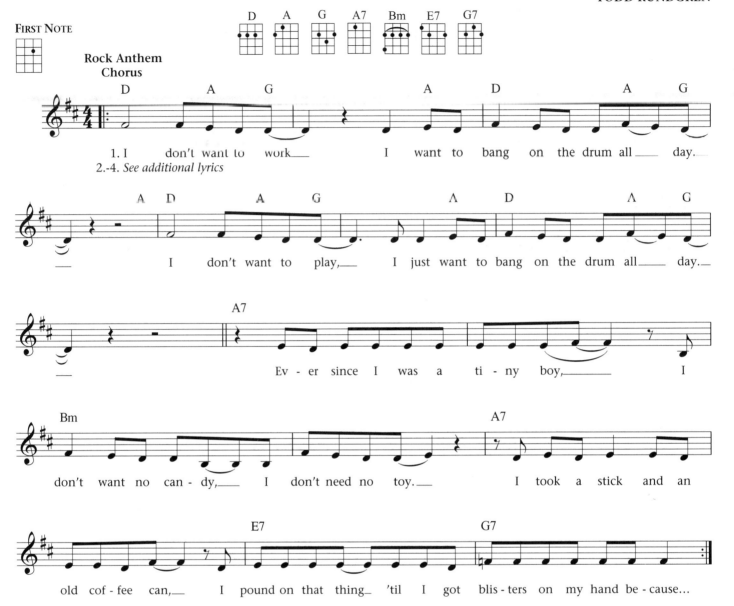

FIRST NOTE

Rock Anthem
Chorus

1. I don't want to work___ I want to bang on the drum all___ day.
2.-4. *See additional lyrics*

___ I don't want to play,___ I just want to bang on the drum all___ day.

Ev - er since I was a ti - ny boy,___ I

don't want no can - dy,___ I don't need no toy.___ I took a stick and an

old cof - fee can,___ I pound on that thing_ 'til I got blis - ters on my hand be - cause...

Additional Lyrics

2. When I get older, they think I'm a fool.
   The teacher told me I should stay after school;
   she caught me pounding on the desk with my hands.
   But my licks was so hot, I made the teacher wanna dance.
   Chorus

3. Every day when I get home from work;
   I feel so frustrated, the boss is a jerk.
   And I get my sticks and go out to the shed
   and I pound on that drum like it was the boss's head because...
   Chorus

Special Extra Verse

4. Well, the weekend comes and my neighbors complain,
   the constant pounding 'bout to drive them insane.
   So I lock up the shed, put my drumsticks away,
   and I sit in the lanai and bang the ukulele daily. Cause-a...
   Chorus

Beyond The Reef

Words and Music by
JACK PITMAN

Slowly

Be - yond the reef,_____ where the sea is dark and cold,_____ my love has

gone,_____ and our dreams grow old. There'll be no tears,_____
Some day I know_____

_____ there'll be no re - gret - ting._____ Will { she / he } re - mem - ber me;_____
_____ { she'll / he'll } come back a - gain to me._____ 'Til then my heart will be_____

Fine

_____ will { she / he } for - get? I'll send a thou - sand flowers,_____ when the trade - winds
_____ be - yond the reef.

D.S. al Fine

blow. I'll send my lone - ly heart,_____ for I love { her / him } so.

(It's A) Beautiful Morning

Words and Music by FELIX CAVALIERE
and EDWARD BRIGATI, JR.

Blue Moon Of Kentucky

Words and Music by
BILL MONROE

Beer Barrel Polka
(Roll Out The Barrel)

By LEW BROWN, WLADIMIR A. TIMM,
JAROMIR VEJVODA and VASEK ZEMAN

There's a gar - den, what a gar - den, on - ly hap - py fac - es bloom there. And there's nev - er an - y room there for a wor - ry or a gloom there. Oh! there's mu - sic and there's danc - ing and a lot of sweet ro - manc - ing. When they play a pol - ka, they all get in the swing: Ev - 'ry time they hear____ that oom - pa - pa;____

hear a rum - ble on the floor;____ ____ ev - 'ry - bod - y feels____ so tra - la - la.____ They want to throw their cares a - ____ it's the big sur - prise____ they're wait - ing for.____ And all the cou - ples form a

way;____ they all go lah - de - ah - de - ay.____ Then they
ring;____ for miles a - round you'll

sing:____ Roll out the bar - rel,____
Zing! Boom! Ta - rar - rel,____

To Coda

we'll have a bar - rel of fun.____ Roll out the
ring out a song of good

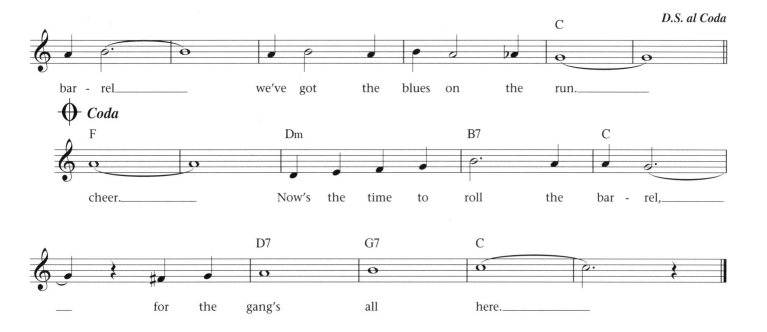

bar - rel_____ we've got the blues on the run._____

Coda

cheer._____ Now's the time to roll the bar - rel,_____

___ for the gang's all here._____

Blues My Naughty Sweetie Gives To Me

**Words and Music by N. SWANSTONE,
CHAS R. McCARRON and CAREY MORGAN**

There are blues that you get from wor - ry.___ There are blues

that you get from pain. And there are blues when you're lone - ly for

your one and on - ly, the blues you can nev - er ex - plain. There are

blues that you get from long - ing,___ but the blu - est blues that

be are the sort of blues that's on my mind,___ they're the ver - y

mean - est kind,___ the blues my naught - y sweet - ie gives___ to me.

Bei Mir Bist Du Schön
(Means That You're Grand)

Original Words by JACOB JACOBS

English Version by SAMMY CAHN
and SAUL CHAPLIN

Music by
SHOLOM SECUNDA

how grand you are.___ I've tried to ex - plain,___ "bei mir bist du schön,"___

___ so, kiss me and say___ you un - der - stand.___

Between The Devil And The Deep Blue Sea

Words by
TED KOEHLER

Music by
HAROLD ARLEN

First Note

Swing

I don't want you, but I'd hate to lose you,
I for - give you, 'cause I can't for - get you,
I should hate you, but I guess I love you,

you've got me

in - be - tween___ the dev - il and the deep blue sea.___

I ought to cross you off my list,___ but when you come knock - ing at my door,___

fate seems to give my heart a twist,_ and I come run - ning back for more.

Coda

dev - il and the deep blue sea.___

Bewitched

Words by
LORENZ HART

Music by
RICHARD RODGERS

1. I'm wild a-gain, be-guiled a-gain, a sim-per-ing, whim-per-ing
2. Could-n't sleep, and would-n't sleep, when love came and told me I

child a-gain; be-witched, both-ered and be-wild-ered am
should-n't sleep; be-witched, both-ered and be-wild-ered am

1. I._____ 2. I._____ Lost my heart, but what of it? He is cold, I a-

gree; he can laugh, but I love it,_____ al-though the laugh's on

me. I'll sing to him, each spring to him, and long for the day when I'll

cling to him; be-witched, both-ered and be-wild-ered am I._____

Black Magic Woman

Words and Music by
PETER GREEN

I got a black mag-ic wom-an,___ I got a black mag-ic wom-an.___

Yes, I got a black mag-ic wom-an, she's got me so blind I can't see, that she's a

black mag-ic wom-an and she's tryin' to make a dev-il out of me.

Don't turn your back on me ba - by;___ don't turn your back on me, ba - by.___

Yes, don't turn your back on me, ba - by, don't mess a - round with your tricks.

Don't turn your back on me, ba - by, you just might pick up my mag-ic sticks.

You got your spell on me, ba - by,___ you got your spell on me, ba - by;___

yes, you got your spell on me, ba - by, turn - in' my heart in - to stone.

I need you so bad,___ mag-ic wom-an, I can't leave you a - lone.

Blue Bayou

Words and Music by
ROY ORBISON and JOE MELSON

Blue Velvet

Words and Music by
BERNIE WAYNE and
LEE MORRIS

Big Girls Don't Cry

Words and Music by
BOB CREWE and BOB GAUDIO

Book Of Love

Words and Music by WARREN DAVIS,
GEORGE MALONE and
CHARLES PATRICK

Boogie Woogie Bugle Boy

Words and Music by DON RAYE
and HUGHIE PRINCE

He makes the comp-'ny jump when he plays re-veil-le, he's the
boo-gie woo-gie bu-gle boy of Com-pa-ny B.___ He Com-pa-ny B.___

Bring Me Sunshine

Words by
SYLVIA DEE

Music by
ARTHUR KENT

Bring me sun-shine___ in your smile;___ bring me
hap - py___ through the years;___ nev - er

laugh - ter___ all the while.___ In this
bring me___ an - y tears.___ Let your

world where we live, there should be more hap - pi - ness___ So much
arms be as warm as the sun from up a - bove,___

joy you can give to each brand new bright to - mor - row! Make me

___ bring me fun,___ bring me sun - shine, bring me love.___

Born Free

Words by
DON BLACK

Music by
JOHN BARRY

Born free,_____ as free as the wind blows,_____ as free as the
Live free,_____ and beau - ty sur - rounds you,_____ the world still as -

grass grows, born free to fol - low your heart.
tounds you, each   time you look at a

star._____ Stay free,_____ where no walls di - vide you,_____ you're free as a

roar - ing tide, so there's no need to___ hide._____ Born free,_____ and life is worth

liv - ing,_____ but on - ly worth liv - ing 'cause you're born free._____

Born To Be Wild

Words and Music by
MARS BONFIRE

Brand New Key

Words and Music by
MELANIE SAFKA

Breaking Up Is Hard To Do

Words and Music by
HOWARD GREENFIELD
and NEIL SEDAKA

Bubbly

Words and Music by
COLBIE CAILLAT and
JASON REEVES

Build Me Up, Buttercup

Words and Music by
TONY McCAULEY and
MICHAEL D'ABO

Bus Stop

Words and Music by
GRAHAM GOULDMAN

California Girls

Words and Music by
BRIAN WILSON and MIKE LOVE

Calendar Girl

Words and Music by
HOWARD GREENFIELD
and NEIL SEDAKA

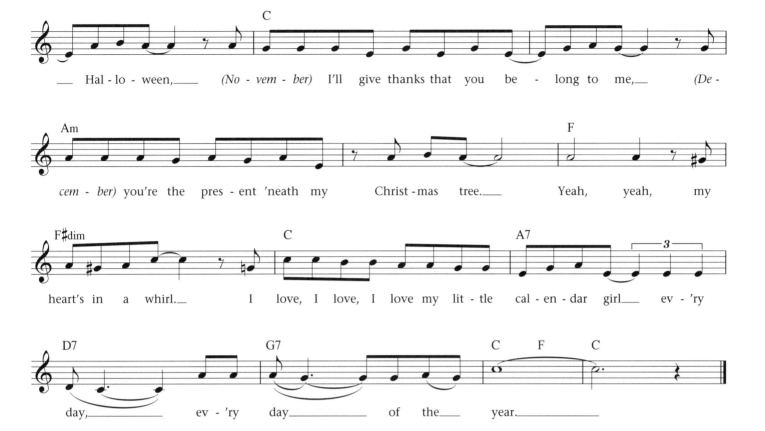

Hal - lo - ween,____ *(No - vem - ber)* I'll give thanks that you be - long to me,____ *(De -*

cem - ber) you're the pres - ent 'neath my Christ - mas tree.____ Yeah, yeah, my

heart's in a whirl.____ I love, I love, I love my lit - tle cal - en - dar girl____ ev - 'ry

day,_____ ev - 'ry day_____ of the____ year._____

59

Call Me

Words and Music by
TONY HATCH

Can't Get Used To Losing You

Words and Music by DOC POMUS
and MORT SHUMAN

Can't Smile Without You

Words and Music by CHRIS ARNOLD,
DAVID MARTIN and
GEOFF MORROW

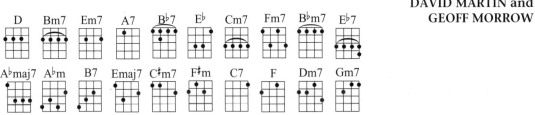

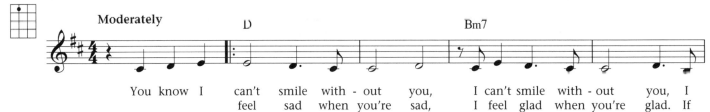

FIRST NOTE

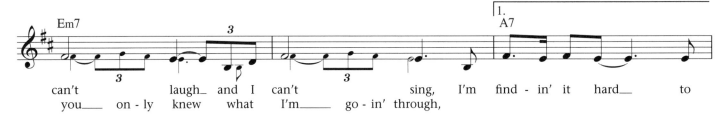

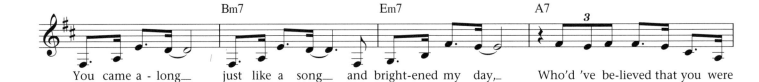

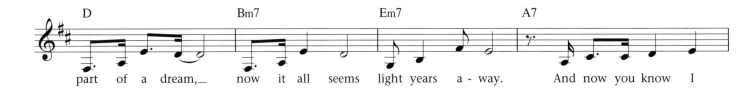

Can't Take My Eyes Off Of You

Words and Music by
**BOB CREWE and
BOB GAUDIO**

Cara Mia

By JULIO TRAPANI
and LEE LANGE

Candy

Words and Music by MACK DAVID,
ALEX KRAMER, and JOAN WHITNEY

Smoothly

"Can - dy," I call my sug - ar "Can - dy," be - cause I'm sweet on

Can - dy and Can - dy's sweet on me._____ {She / He} un - der - stands me, Can - dy,

my un - der - stand - ing Can - dy, and Can - dy's al - ways hand - y
it's gon - na be just dan - dy, the day I take my Can - dy

when I need sym - pa - thy._____ I wish that there were
and make {her / him} mine all mine._____

four of { her,___ / him,___ } so I could love much more of { her.___ / him.___ }

{She / He} has tak - en my com - plete heart, got a sweet tooth for my sweet-heart.

Catch A Falling Star

Words and Music by PAUL VANCE
and LEE POCKRISS

67

Catch The Wind

Words and Music by
DONOVAN LEITCH

Could I Have This Dance

Words and Music by
WAYLAND HOLYFIELD
and BOB HOUSE

Cecilia

Words and Music by
PAUL SIMON

fall on the floor___ and I'm laugh - ing.___ Ju - bi - ing.___ Oh, oh,___

___ oh, oh, oh, oh, oh, oh, oh,___ oh, oh, oh, oh, oh, oh, oh, oh,___

___ oh.___ Oh oh,___ ___ oh.___ Come on home.___

Carolina Moon

Words and Music by
BENNY DAVIS and JOE BURKE

FIRST NOTE

Slowly

1. Car - o - lin - a moon keep shin - ing,
2. Car - o - lin - a moon I'm pin - ing,
3. Tell her that I'm blue and lone - ly,

To Coda

shin - ing on the one___ who waits for me.___
pin - ing for the place___ I long to be.___ ___ How I'm
dream - y Car - o -

hop - ing to - night you'll go, go to the right win - dow, scat - ter your light,

D.C. al Coda   Coda

say I'm all right, please do.___   lin - a moon.___

Cherish

Words and Music by
TERRY KIRKMAN

me. That have the right a-mount of let-ters, just the right sound, that could

make you hear, make you see that you are driv-ing me out of my mind.

Oh, I could say I need you, but then you'd re-a-lize that I want you. Just like a

thou-sand oth-er guys who'd say they loved you with all the rest of their lies when all they

D.C. al Coda
(1st verse)

want-ed was to touch your face, your hands, and gaze in-to your eyes.

Coda

Cher-ish me as much as I cher-ish you. And I

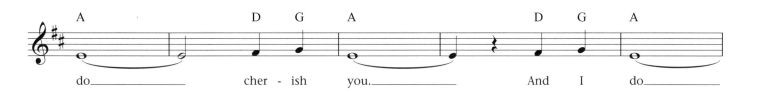

do cher-ish you. And I do

cher-ish you. Cher-ish is the word.

Circle Of Life

Words by
TIM RICE

Music by
ELTON JOHN

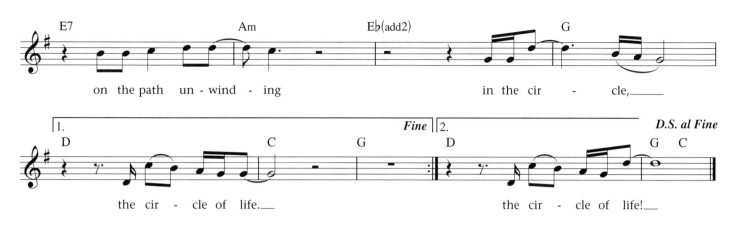

on the path un-wind-ing   in the cir - cle,_____

1. the cir - cle of life.___   *Fine*   2. the cir - cle of life!___   *D.S. al Fine*

Come Go With Me

Words and Music by
C.E. QUICK

Love, love me dar - lin; come and go___ with me.___ Please don't send me

'way be - yond___ the sea.___ I need you dar - lin', so come go___ with me.___

Come, come, come, come, come in - to___ my heart.___ Tell me, dar - lin',

we will nev - er part.___ I need you, dar - lin', so come go___ with

me._____ Yes, I need you, yes, I real - ly need you;

please say you'll nev - er leave me. Well say, you nev - er

yes, you real - ly nev - er; you nev - er give me a chance.

Come Monday

Words and Music by
JIMMY BUFFETT

Come Saturday Morning
(Saturday Morning)

Words by
DORY PREVIN

Music by
FRED KARLIN

Crocodile Rock

**Words and Music by ELTON JOHN
and BERNIE TAUPIN**

bet - ter time___ and I guess___ I nev - er___ will.___ Oh,___

B7 ___ lawd - y, ma - ma, those Fri - day nights when Su - sie wore___ her dress - es tight___ and E7

A7 the Croc - o - dile Rock - in' was a - out_____ of a sight._____ G

To Coda ⊕ D La,_____ la, la, la, la la,_____ la, la, la, la, Bm7

G la.___ La, la, la, la, la. 1. 2. But the years___ *D.S. al Coda* 3. I re - mem - A7

⊕ *Coda* La,___ la, la, la, la, la._____ La, la, la, la, D Bm7

G la._____ La, la, la, la, la. *Repeat and fade* A7

79

Crying In The Rain

A Day In The Life Of A Fool
(Manhã de Carnaval)

Words by
CARL SIGMAN

Music by
LUIZ BONFÁ

Dancing In The Street

Words and Music by
**MARVIN GAYE, IVY HUNTER
and WILLIAM STEVENSON**

Delilah

Words and Music by
LES REED and BARRY MASON

Don't Fence Me In

Words and Music by
COLE PORTER

Do You Believe In Magic

Words and Music by
JOHN SEBASTIAN

FIRST NOTE

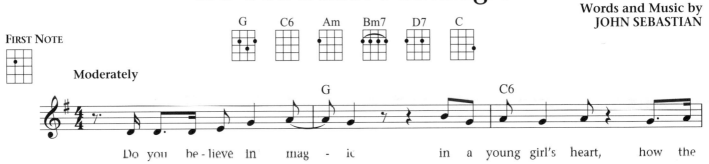

Moderately

Do you be-lieve in mag - ic   in a young girl's heart,   how the

mu - sic can   free her when - ev - er it starts?   And it's mag - ic   if the

mu - sic is groov - y,   it makes you feel hap - py like an old time mov - ie.   I'll

tell   you 'bout the mag - ic and   a - free   your soul,   but it's like

try - in' to tell a stran - ger 'bout a - rock and   roll._____

If you be-lieve in mag - ic,   don't___ both - er to choose,   if it's
ic   come a - long with___ me,   we'll___

jug band___ mu - sic   or rhy - thm and blues.   Just go and
dance un - til morn - ing 'til there's just you and me.   And___

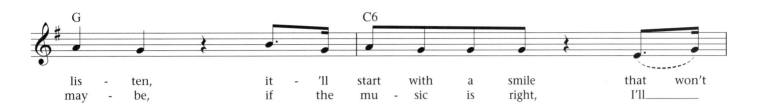

lis - ten,   it - 'll start with a smile   that won't
may - be,   if the mu - sic is right,   I'll_____

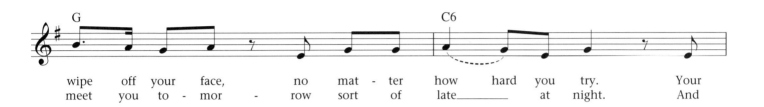

wipe off your face,   no mat - ter how hard you try.   Your
meet you to - mor - row sort of late_____ at night.   And

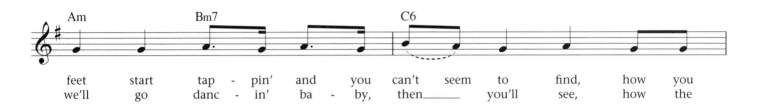

feet start tap - pin' and you can't seem to find, how you
we'll go danc - in' ba - by, then_____ you'll see, how the

got there; so just blow your mind._____

If you be - lieve in mag - mag - ic's in the mu - sic and the

mu - sic's in me._____ Yeah!   Do you be - lieve like

Repeat and Fade

I be - lieve? Do you be - lieve like I be - lieve? Do

Do You Know The Way To San Jose

Lyric by
HAL DAVID

Music by
BURT BACHARACH

Do You Know What It Means To Miss New Orleans

Words and Music by
EDDIE DE LANGE and LOUIS ALTER

(Sittin' On) The Dock Of The Bay

Words and Music by STEVE CROPPER
and OTIS REDDING

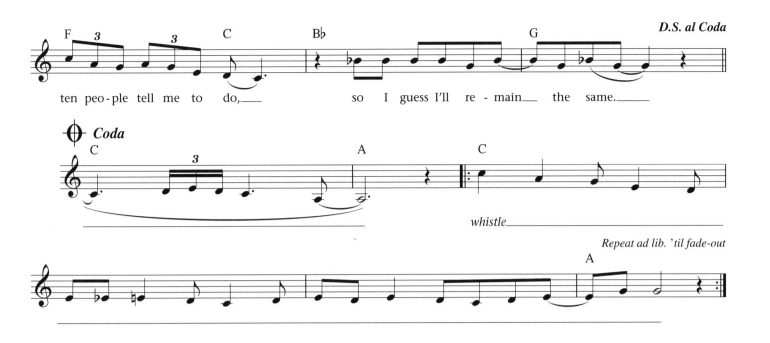

ten peo - ple tell me to do,___ so I guess I'll re - main___ the same.___

Coda

whistle_____

Repeat ad lib. 'til fade-out

'Deed I Do

Words and Music by
WALTER HIRSCH and FRED ROSE

Do I___ want you?___ Oh my,___ do I?
Do I___ need you?___ Oh my,___ do I?
Do I___ love you?___ Oh my,___ do I?

Hon - ey,___ 'deed I do!___
Hon - ey,___ 'deed I do!___
Hon - ey,___ 'deed I

I'm glad that I'm the one who found you, that's why I'm

al - ways hang - in' 'round you. do!___

Don't Let The Sun Catch You Crying

Words and Music by GERARD MARSDEN,
FRED MARSDEN, LES CHADWICK
and LES MAGUIRE

Don't Worry Baby

Words and Music by BRIAN WILSON
and ROGER CHRISTIAN

FIRST NOTE

F Bb C7 Gm7 Am D7 G

Moderate Rock

F   Bb

1. Well,___ it's been build-in' up in-side of me for, oh, I don't know
2. I___ guess I should-a kept my mouth shut when I start-ed to brag a-
3. She___ told me "Ba-by, when you race to-day, just take a-long my

C7   F

how___ long.   I___ don't know why, but I keep think-in'
bout___ my car.   But___ I can't back___ down now be-cause I
love___ with you.   And___ if you knew how much I loved you, ba-by,

Bb   C7   Gm7

some-thing's bound___ to go___ wrong.   But she looks
pushed the oth-er guys___ too far.   She makes me
noth-ing could___ go wrong___ with you."   Oh, what she

To Coda ⊕

C7   Am   D7   G

in my eyes___ and makes me re-al-ize___ when she says:_____ ⎫
come a-live___ and makes me wan-na drive___ when she says:_____ ⎬
does to me___ when she makes love to me___ and she says:_____ ⎭

Am   D7

Don't wor-ry, ba-by,___ ev-'ry-thing will turn

G   Am   D7   **1.** C7   **2.** *D.C. al Coda* C7

out all___ right. Don't wor-ry, ba-by,___ ooh.___   ooh.___

⊕ *Coda*

Am   D7   G

Don't wor-ry, ba-by,___ ev-'ry-thing will turn out all___ right. Don't wor-ry,

Don't Pass Me By

Words and Music by
RICHARD STARKEY

self;___ I don't see you. Does it mean___ you don't
two.___ I said that's all right, I'm wait - ing here,_____ just

love me an - y - more?___
wait - ing to hear from you.___

Don't pass me by,___ don't make me cry, don't make me blue,___

___ 'cause you know dar - ling, I

love on - ly you.___ You'll nev - er

know it hurt me so.___ How I hate to see you go;___

___ don't pass me by,___ don't make me

cry.___

1.

2.

I'm

Don't Think Twice, It's All Right

Words and Music by
BOB DYLAN

Don't Stop

Words and Music by
CHRISTINE McVIE

Down At The Twist And Shout

Words and Music by
MARY CHAPIN CARPENTER

High - way 10, past a - La - fay - ette, there's a
here up north, it's a cold, cold rain and there
learn to dance with your rock 'n' roll, you

Bat - on Rouge. And I won't for - get to send you a card with
ain't no cure for my blues to - day; ex - cept when the pa - per says
learn to swing with do - si - do. But you learn to love at the

D.C. al Fine
(4th time)

my re - grets 'cause I'm nev - er gon - na come back home.
Beau - so - leil is a com - in' in - to town. Ba - by, let's go down. It's
fais do do when you hear a lit - tle Jo - lie Blon.

Dream

Words and Music by
JOHNNY MERCER

FIRST NOTE

Slow and Dreamy

Dream when you're feel - in' blue; dream
dream when the day is thru; dream

that's the thing to do. Just watch the smoke - rings
and they might come true. Things nev - er are as

1.
rise in the air, you'll find your share of mem - o - ries there. So

2.
bad as they seem, so dream, dream, dream.

Down In The Boondocks

Words and Music by
JOE SOUTH

Down On The Corner

Words and Music by
JOHN FOGERTY

Dream Baby
(How Long Must I Dream)

Words and Music by
CINDY WALKER

Sweet dream, ba - by. Sweet dream, ba - by. Sweet
dream, ba - by. How long must I dream?___ Dream ba - by got___
___ me dream-in' sweet dreams the whole day through. Dream ba - by got___
___ me dream - in' sweet dreams, night - time too. I love you and___
___ I'm dream-in' of you, that won't do.___ Dream ba - by, make___
___ me stop my dream - in', you can make my dreams___ come true. Oh,___ true.

Dream Lover

Words and Music by
BOBBY DARIN

Down Under

Words and Music by
COLIN HAY and RON STRYKERT

1. Tra - vel - ing in a fried - out Kom - bi
2. Buy - ing bread from a man in Brus - sels, he was
3. Ly - ing in a den in Bom - bay

on a hip - py trail head full of zom - bie.
six - foot - four and full of mus - cles.
with a slack - jaw and not much to say.

I met a strange la - dy, she made me ner - vous;
I said "Do you speak - a my lan - guage?"
I said to the man, "Are you tryin' to tempt me?

she took me in and gave me break - fast. And she said,
He just smiled and gave me a Veg - e - mite sand - wich. And he said,
Be - cause I come from the land of plen - ty." And he said,

1., 3. "Do you come from a land down un - der,
2. I come from a land down un - der,

where wom - en glow and men plun - der?
where beer does flow and men chun - der.

Can't you hear, can't you hear the thun - der? You

Last time D.S. and Fade

bet - ter run, you bet - ter take cov - er.

Drifting And Dreaming
(Sweet Paradise)

Words by
HAVEN GILLESPIE

Music by EGBERT VAN ALSTYNE,
ERWIN R. SCHMIDT and LOYAL CURTIS

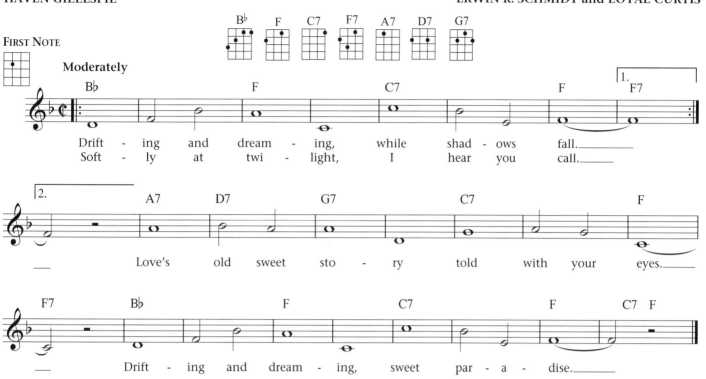

FIRST NOTE

Moderately

Drift - ing and dream - ing, while shad - ows fall.____
Soft - ly at twi - light, I hear you call.____

Love's old sweet sto - ry told with your eyes.____

Drift - ing and dream - ing, sweet par - a - dise.____

Duke Of The Uke

Words and Music by
DAVE FRANKLIN and
PERRY BOTKIN

Duke of the Uke,_____ Duke of the Uke_____ plays with the band out there on the sand, the Duke of the Uke. He's got a beat;_____ plays hot or sweet,_____ the Duke plays the uke and the boys and the girls sing a song,_____ a song of love. Fare - well to thee, it's plain to see, he's roy - al - ty in old Wai - ki - ki. He makes you dance,_____ start a ro - mance._____ Come on and meet the Duke of the Uke with me.

The End Of The World

Words by
SYLVIA DEE

Music by
ARTHUR KENT

Elenore

Words and Music by JOHN BARBATA,
HOWARD KAYLAN, AL NICHOL,
JIM PONS and MARK VOLMAN

Everyday

Words and Music by NORMAN PETTY
and CHARLES HARDIN

Every Breath You Take

Music and Lyrics by
STING

I keep cry - ing ba - by, ba - by please.____

D.S. al Coda

Oh, can't you____

Coda

Ev - 'ry move_ you make ev - 'ry step_ you take, I'll be watch -ing you.

Repeat and Fade

I'll be watch - ing you.____

Everybody's Talkin'
(Echoes)

Words and Music by
FRED NEIL

Exactly Like You

Words by
DOROTHY FIELDS

Music by
JIMMY McHUGH

1. I know why I've wait-ed, know why I've been blue;
2. Why should we spend mon-ey on a show or two?

prayed each night for some-one ex-act-ly like you.____
No one does those love scenes ex-act-ly like you.__

You make me feel so grand.____ I want to hand the world to you.____

You seem to un-der-stand____ each fool-ish lit-tle scheme I'm schem-ing,

dream I'm dream-ing. Now I know why moth-er taught me to be

true. She meant me for some-one ex-act-ly like you.____

Everything Is Beautiful

Words and Music by
RAY STEVENS

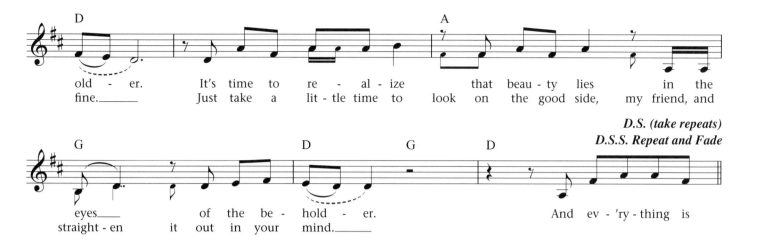

D.S. (take repeats)
D.S.S. Repeat and Fade

Falling In Love Again
(Can't Help It)

Words by
SAMMY LERNER

Music by
FREDERICK HOLLANDER

1. Fall - ing in love a - gain, nev - er want - ed to.
2. Love's al - ways been my game, play it how I may.

What am I to do? Can't help it!
I was made that way. Can't help it!

Men / Girls clus - ter to me like moths a - round a flame. And if their

wings burn, I know I'm not to blame. Fall - ing in love a - gain,

nev - er want - ed to. What am I to do? Can't help it!

Falling Slowly

Words and Music by GLEN HANSARD
and MARKETA IRGLOVA

Ferry 'Cross The Mersey

Wordds and Music by
GERARD MARSDEN

Fever

Words and Music by
JOHN DAVENPORT
and EDDIE COOLEY

Additional Lyrics

3. Romeo loved Juliet,
Juliet she felt the same.
When he put his arms around her, he said,
"Julie, baby, you're my flame."

Thou givest fever, when we kisseth,
fever with thy flaming youth.
Fever—I'm afire,
fever, yes I burn forsooth.

4. Captain Smith and Pocahontas
had a very mad affair.
When her Daddy tried to kill him, she said,
"Daddy-o don't you dare."

Give me fever with his kisses,
fever when he holds me tight.
Fever—I'm his Missus;
oh Daddy, won't you treat him right?

5. Now you've listened to my story,
here's the point that I have made:
Chicks were born to give you fever,
be it fahrenheit or centigrade.

They give you fever when you kiss them,
fever if you live and learn.
Fever—'til you sizzle;
what a lovely way to burn.

Fly Me To The Moon
(In Other Words)

Words and Music by
BART HOWARD

Fly me to the moon, and let me play a - mong the stars; let me see what spring is like on Ju - pi - ter and Mars. In oth - er words, hold my hand! In oth - er words, dar - ling, kiss me! Fill my heart with song, and let me sing for - ev - er - more; you are all I long for, all I wor - ship and a - dore. In oth - er words, please be true! In oth - er words, I love

1. you!

2. true! In oth - er words, I love you!

Forever Young

Words and Music by
BOB DYLAN

Five Hundred Miles

Words and Music by
HEDY WEST

From A Distance

Words and Music by
JULIE GOLD

G   Em   Am   D7   G   D7

watch-ing us,   God_ is watch-ing us   from a dis - tance.___   From a

Coda

C   D7   Em   C   G

heart___ of ev - 'ry___ man.   It's the hope of__ hopes,___ it's the

C   G   C   D7   G   C   D7   G

love of__ loves,___ it's the song of ev - 'ry man.

Freight Train

**Words and Music by
ELIZABETH COTTEN**

FIRST NOTE

C   G7   E7   F

Moderately

C   G7

1. Freight train, freight train, run so fast,___
2. When I'm dead and in my grave,___
3. When I die, Lord bur - y me deep;___

C

freight train, freight train, run so fast.___
no more good times here I'll crave.___
way down on old Chest - nut Street.___

E7   F

Please   don't tell what__ train I'm on,___ they won't
Place   the stones at my head and feet;___ tell them
Then I can hear old__ Num - ber Nine___ as

C   G7   C

Repeat 1st verse last time

know what__ route I've gone.
all that I've gone to sleep.
she comes__ roll - ing by.

For All We Know

Words by
SAM M. LEWIS

Music by
J. FRED COOTS

Fun, Fun, Fun

Words and Music by BRIAN WILSON
and MIKE LOVE

Garden Song

Words and Music by
DAVE MALLETT

FIRST NOTE

Moderately, in 2

1., 4. Inch by inch,_____ row by row,_____ gon-na make this gar-
2. Pull-ing weeds_ and pick-in' stones,_ man is made_ of dreams_
3. Plant your rows_____ straight and long;_ tem-per them_ with prayer_

-den grow._ All it takes is a rake and a hoe and a
_ and bones._ Feel the need to grow my own_ 'cause the
_ and song._ Moth-er Earth will make you strong_ if you

piece of_ fer-tile ground.__ Inch by inch, row by row,__
time is_ close at hand.__ Grain for grain, sun and rain,_
give her_ love and care.__ Old crow watch-ing hun-gri-ly_

some-one bless these seeds I sow._ Some-one warm them from be-low 'til the
find my way in na-ture's chain,_ tune my bod-y and my brain to the
from his perch in yon-der tree._ In my gar-den, I'm as free as that

3rd time D.C. al Coda
(take verse 4)

⊕ **Coda**

rain comes tum-bl-ing down.
mu-sic from the land.__
feath-ered thief up there.__

rain comes tum-bl-ing down.

Girl

Words and Music by JOHN LENNON
and PAUL McCARTNEY

Goin' Out Of My Head

Words and Music by TEDDY RANDAZZO
and BOBBY WEINSTEIN

Good Riddance
(Time Of Your Life)

Groovin'

Words and Music by
FELIX CAVALIERE and
EDWARD BRIGATI, JR.

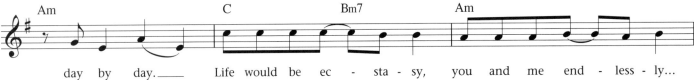

Goodnight, My Someone

Words and Music by
MEREDITH WILLSON

The Great Pretender

Words and Music by
BUCK RAM

Hallelujah

Words and Music by
LEONARD COHEN

Happy Days Are Here Again

Words by
JACK YELLEN

Music by
MILTON AGER

Hello! Ma Baby

Words by
IDA EMERSON

Music by
JOSEPH E. HOWARD

Hello Mary Lou

Words and Music by GENE PITNEY and C. MANGIARACINA

Hanalei Moon

Words and Music by
BOB NELSON

FIRST NOTE

Slowly, with feeling

When you see Ha - na - lei by moon - light,_____ you will
breeze, ev - 'ry wave will whis - per;_____ "You are

be in hea - ven_____ by the sea. Ev - 'ry way."
mine. Don't ev - er_____ go a -

Ha - na - lei, Ha - na - lei moon is light - ing_____ be - lov - ed_____ Kau -

a - 'i._____ Ha - na - lei, Ha - na - lei moon. A -

lo - ha no wau i - a o - e._____ A - o - e_____ Ha - na - lei moon.

The Hawaiian Turnaround

Words by
JIM BELOFF

Music by
HERB OHTA

1. When you ar - rive___ in Hon - no - lu - lu, there's an un - mis -
2. No - ta - ble notes,___ you hear 'em at the start and end of
3. When you get home,___ the mo - ment that your feet are fin - 'lly

tak - a - ble sound.___ Ev - 'ry - where that mu - sic is found,___
man - y a song.___ And you'll find you're hum - ming a - long;___
touch - ing the ground,___ in your heart you're par - a - dise bound;___

it's the Ha - wai - ian turn - a - round.
it's the Ha - wai - ian turn - a - round.
it's the Ha - wai - ian turn - a - round.

Beau - ti - ful views,___ ev - 'ry di - rec - tion.___ Trop - i - cal hues,___

pic - ture per - fec - tion;_ par - a - dise found,_ each time you turn_ a - round.

This is the Ha - wai - ian turn - a - round.

137

Have You Ever Seen The Rain?

Words and Music by
JOHN FOGERTY

138

Heatwave
(Love Is Like A Heatwave)

Words and Music by
EDWARD HOLLAND, LAMONT DOZIER
and BRIAN HOLLAND

Hey, Soul Sister

Words and Music by PAT MONAHAN,
ESPEN LIND and AMUND BJORKLAND

High Hopes

Words by
SAMMY CAHN

Music by
JIMMY VAN HEUSEN

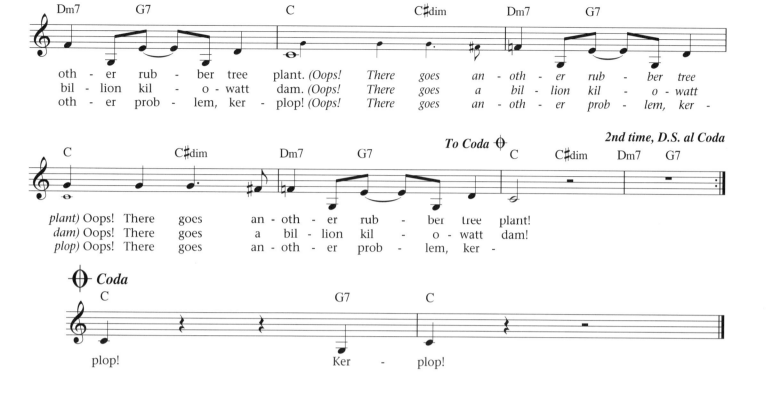

| Dm7 | G7 | | C | C#dim | Dm7 | G7 |

oth - er rub - ber tree plant. *(Oops! There goes an - oth - er rub - ber tree*
bil - lion kil - o - watt dam. *(Oops! There goes a bil - lion kil - o - watt*
oth - er prob - lem, ker - plop! *(Oops! There goes an - oth - er prob - lem, ker -*

To Coda ⊕   ***2nd time, D.S. al Coda***

| C | C#dim | Dm7 | G7 | C | C#dim | Dm7 | G7 |

plant) Oops! There goes an - oth - er rub - ber tree plant!
dam) Oops! There goes a bil - lion kil - o - watt dam!
plop) Oops! There goes an - oth - er prob - lem, ker -

⊕ **Coda**

| C | | G7 | C |

plop!   Ker - plop!

Homeward Bound

Words and Music by
PAUL SIMON

Additional Lyrics

2. Every day's an endless stream
   of cigarettes and magazines.
   And each town looks the same to me,
   the movies and the factories;
   and every stranger's face I see
   reminds me that I long to be...
   Chorus

3. Tonight I'll sing my songs again,
   I'll play the game and pretend.
   But all my words come back to me
   in shades of mediocrity,
   like emptiness in harmony,
   I need someone to comfort me.
   Chorus

Honeycomb

Words and Music by
BOB MERRILL

Honey Pie

Words and Music by JOHN LENNON
and PAUL McCARTNEY

knee.
me. T - t - tee.___ Oh, Hon-ey Pie,___ you are driv - ing me
Now, Hon-ey Pie,___ you are mak - ing me

fran - tic.___ Sail a - cross___ the At - lan - tic,
cra - zy.___ I'm in love___ but I'm la - zy,

1.
to be where you be - long.___ Hon-ey Pie, come back to___ me.
so won't you please come___ home.___

2.
___ Come, come back to me, Hon-ey Pie. Ha___ ha ha.___

Oo,___ Oo,___

Hon - ey Pie, Hon - ey Pie.

Hey, Look Me Over

Words by
CAROLYN LEIGH

Music by
CY COLEMAN

Hey, look me o-ver, lend me an ear; fresh out of clo-ver,
mort-gaged up to here.___ But don't pass the plate, folks, don't pass the cup;___ I
fig-ure when-ev-er you're down and out, the on-ly way is up. And I'll be
up like a rose-bud, high on the vine; don't thumb your nose, bud, take a tip from
mine. I'm a lit-tle bit short of the el-bow room, but let me get me
some, {and look out, / hear me shout,} world, here I come. 'come.___

Honeysuckle Rose

Words by
ANDY RAZAF

Music by
THOMAS "FATS" WALLER

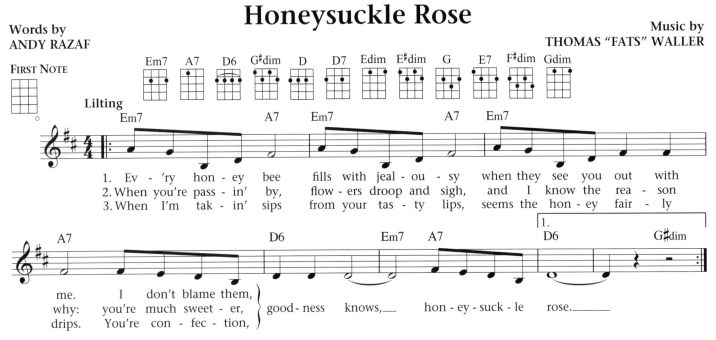

1. Ev - 'ry hon - ey bee fills with jeal - ou - sy when they see you out with
2. When you're pass - in' by, flow - ers droop and sigh, and I know the rea - son
3. When I'm tak - in' sips from your tas - ty lips, seems the hon - ey fair - ly

me. I don't blame them,
why: you're much sweet - er, {good - ness knows,___ hon - ey - suck - le rose.___
drips. You're con - fec - tion,

Hooked On A Feeling

**Words and Music by
MARK JAMES**

© 1968 (Renewed 1996) SCREEN GEMS-EMI MUSIC INC.

149

Honolulu Baby

Words and Music by
MARVIN HATLEY

Hot Diggity (Dog Ziggity Boom)

Words and Music by AL HOFFMAN
and DICK MANNING

G D7 Am B7 E7 A7

First Note

Moderately bright Waltz

Hot dig-gi-ty dog zig-gi-ty boom, what you do to me! It's so

new to me, what you do to me. Hot dig-gi-ty dog zig-gi-ty boom, what you

To Coda

do to me! When you're hold-ing me tight!

Nev-er dreamed an-y-
Nev-er knew that my
There's a cute lit-tle

bod-y could kiss that-a-way, bring me bliss that-a-way, with a
heart could go "Zing!" that-a-way, ting-a-ling that-a-way, make me
cot-tage for two, that-a-way, skies are blue that-a-way, dreams come

kiss that-a-way._____ What a won-der-ful feel-ing to
sing that-a-way._____ Said "Good-bye" to my trou-bles, they
true that-a-way._____ If you say I can share it with

3rd time, D.C. al Coda

feel that-a-way, tell me where have you been all my life? Oh!
went that-a-way, ev-er since you came in-to my life! Oh!
you, that-a-way, I'll be hap-py the rest of my life! Oh!

Coda

How my fu-ture will shine_____ from the mo-ment you're mine!

I Can't Help But Wonder
(Where I'm Bound)

Words and Music by
TOM PAXTON

FIRST NOTE

Moderately

1. It's a long and dust-y road; it's a hot and a heav-y load, and the
2. I have been a-round this land just a do in' the best I can, try-in' to
3. *See additional lyrics*

folks I meet ain't al-ways kind. Some are bad and some are good, some have
find what I was meant to do. And the fac-es that I see are as

done the best they could; some have tried to ease my trou-bl-in'
wor-ried as can be, and it looks like they are won-der-in'

mind.)
too.) And I can't help but won-der where I'm bound, where I'm bound. And I

can't help but won-der where I'm bound.____

Additional Lyrics

3. I had a little gal one time,
   she had lips like sherry wine.
   And she loved me 'til my head went plumb insane.
   But I was too blind to see,
   she was driftin' away from me,
   and one day she left on the morning train.
   Chorus

4. I've got a buddy from home,
   but he started out to roam.
   And I hear he's out by 'Frisco Bay.
   And sometimes when I've had a few,
   his voice comes singin' through.
   And I'm goin' out to see him some old day.
   Chorus

5. If you see me passing by,
   and you sit and wonder why;
   and you wish that you were a rambler, too.
   Nail your shoes to the kitchen floor;
   lace 'em up and bar the door.
   Thank your stars for the roof that's over you.
   Chorus

I Don't Care If The Sun Don't Shine

Words and Music by
MACK DAVID

I Got You Babe

Words and Music by
SONNY BONO

I Just Called To Say I Love You

Words and Music by
STEVIE WONDER

I Heard It Through The Grapevine

Words and Music by
NORMAN J. WHITFIELD
and BARRETT STRONG

heard it through the grape - vine.   Oh,_____   I'm just
_____ it through the grape - vine.   And I'm   just

a - bout to lose_____ my mind._____ Hon - ey, hon - ey, oh
a - bout to lose_____ my mind._____ (I

yeah.
heard it through the grape - vine, not much long - er would you be mine, ba -

To Coda ⊕ 1.   2.

- *by.)*

Ooh._____   I know a man_   _____   Ooh._____
Ooh._
Yeah._

D.S. al Coda
(See addtional lyrics)

Peo - ple say be - lieve half_____

⊕ *Coda*

_____ yeah, yeah,_____ yeah.   I heard it through the grape - vine, not much

Repeat and Fade

long - er would you be mine, ba - by.   Yeah,

Additional Lyrics

3. People say believe half of what you see,
oh, and none of what you hear.
But I can't help but be confused,
if it's true please tell me dear.
Do you plan to let me go
for the other guy you loved before?

I Love How You Love Me

I Only Want To Be With You

Words and Music by
MIKE HAWKER and
IVOR RAYMONDE

I Saw The Light

Words and Music by
TODD RUNDGREN

Coda

And I ran out be-fore,___ but I won't___ do it an-y-more.___ Can't you see___ the light___ in my eyes?___ In my___ eyes,___ in my___

Repeat and Fade

I Don't Know Why (I Just Do)

Lyric by
ROY TURK

Music by
FRED E. AHLERT

FIRST NOTE

Slowly

I don't know why___ I love you like I do.___ I don't know why,___ I just do. I don't know why___ you thrill me like you do.___ I don't know why,___ you just do. You nev-er seem to want my ro-manc - ing; the on-ly time you hold me is when we're danc - ing. I don't know why___ I love you like I do.___ I don't know why,___ I just do.

I Think We're Alone Now

Words and Music by
RITCHIE CORDELL

I Wanna Be Free

Words and Music by
TOMMY BOYCE and BOBBY HART

I Want You Back

Words and Music by FREDDIE PERREN,
ALPHONSO MIZELL, BERRY GORDY
and DEKE RICHARDS

I Whistle A Happy Tune

Words by
OSCAR HAMMERSTEIN II

Music by
RICHARD RODGERS

I Wish You Love

English Words by
ALBERT BEACH

French Words and Music by
CHARLES TRENET

I Will Survive

Words and Music by
DINO FEKARIS and
FREDERICK J. PERREN

I'll Never Fall In Love Again

Words by
HAL DAVID

Music by
BURT BACHARACH

I Want To Be Happy

Words by
IRVING CAESAR

Music by
VINCENT YOUMANS

I'll Never Find Another You

Words and Music by
TOM SPRINGFIELD

I'll See You In My Dreams

Words by
GUS KAHN

Music by
ISHAM JONES

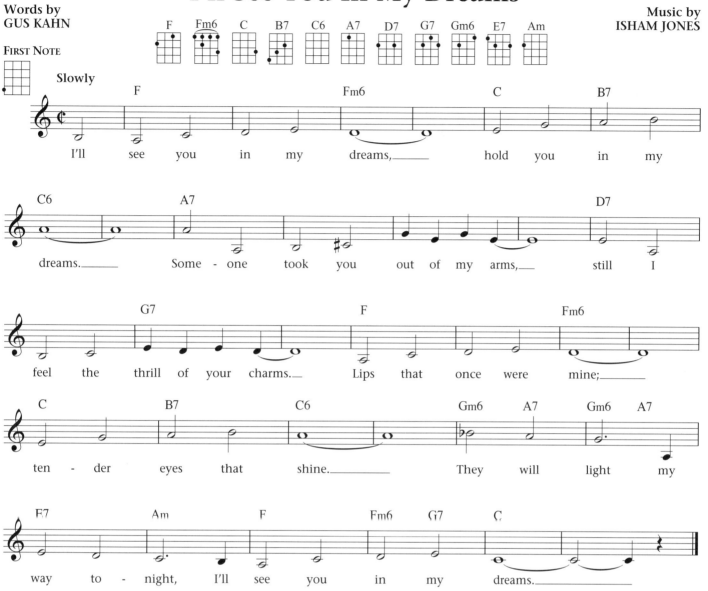

I'll see you in my dreams,_____ hold you in my dreams._____ Some - one took you out of my arms,___ still I feel the thrill of your charms.___ Lips that once were mine;_____ ten - der eyes that shine._____ They will light my way to - night, I'll see you in my dreams._____

I'm An Old Cowhand
(From The Rio Grande)

Words and Music by
JOHNNY MERCER

I'm Confessin' (That I Love You)

Words and Music by AL NEIBURG,
DOC DAUGHERTY and ELLIS REYNOLDS

I'm Gonna Sit Right Down And
Write Myself A Letter

Lyric by
JOE YOUNG

Music by
FRED E. AHLERT

I'm Into Something Good

Words and Music by
GERRY GOFFIN and CAROLE KING

I'm Thinking Tonight Of My Blue Eyes

Words and Music by
A.P. CARTER

I've Got My Love To Keep Me Warm

Words and Music by
IRVING BERLIN

If We Only Have Love
(Quand On N'a Que L'amour)

English Words by
MORT SHUMAN and ERIC BLAU

French Words and Music by
JACQUES BREL

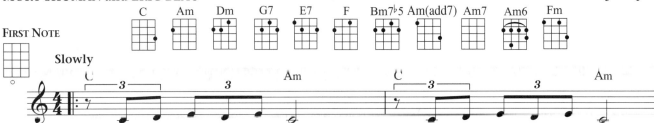

1. If we on - ly have love, then to - mor - row will dawn;
2. If we on - ly have love, we can reach those in pain;

and the days of our years will rise on that morn. If we on - ly have love
we can heal all our wounds, we can use our own names. If we on - ly have love,

to em - brace with - out fears; we will kiss with our eyes, we will sleep with - out tears.
we can melt all the guns; and then give the new world to our daugh - ters and sons.

If we on - ly have love, with our arms o - pened wide; then the young and the old
If we on - ly have love, then Je - ru - sa - lem stands; and then death has no shad - ow,

will stand at our side. If we on - ly have love, love that's fall - ing like rain;
there are no for - eign lands. If we on - ly have love, we will nev - er bow down;

then the parched des - ert earth will grow green a - gain. If we on - ly have love,
we'll be tall as the pines, nei - ther he - roes nor clowns. If we on - ly have love,

for the hymn that we shout; for the song that we sing, then we'll have a way
then we'll on - ly be men; and we'll drink from the Grail, to be born once a -

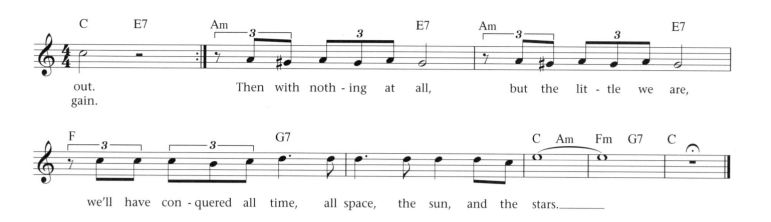

out.
gain.

Then with noth-ing at all, but the lit-tle we are,

we'll have con-quered all time, all space, the sun, and the stars._____

I'm Looking Over A Four Leaf Clover

Lyric by
MORT DIXON

Music by
HARRY WOODS

I'm look-ing o-ver a four leaf clo-ver that I o-ver-looked be-

fore:_____ one leaf is sun-shine, the sec-ond is rain,_____ third is the

ros-es that grow in the lane._____ No need ex-plain-ing, the one re-main-

-ing is some-bod-y I a-dore._____ I'm look-ing o-ver a

four leaf clo-ver that I o-ver-looked be-fore._____

If You Want To Sing Out, Sing Out

Words and Music by
YUSUF ISLAM

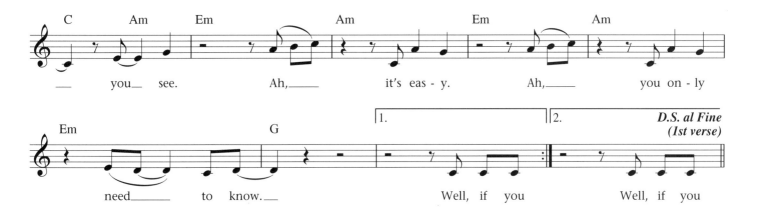

you_ see. Ah,_____ it's eas - y. Ah,_____ you on - ly

need_____ to know._____ Well, if you Well, if you

I'm Sitting On Top Of The World

Words by SAM M. LEWIS
and JOE YOUNG

Music by
RAY HENDERSON

I'm sit - ting on top of the world,_____ just roll - ing a -
quit - ting the blues of the world,_____ just sing - ing a

long,_____ just roll - ing a - long._____ I'm
song,_____ just sing - ing a - song._____ "Glo - ry hal - le - lu - jah,"

I just phoned the Par - son, "Hey, Par get read - y to call." Just like Hump - ty

Dump - ty, I'm go - ing to fall. I'm sit - ting on top of the

world,_____ just roll - ing a - long,_____ just roll - ing a - long.

The "In" Crowd

Words and Music by
BILLY PAGE

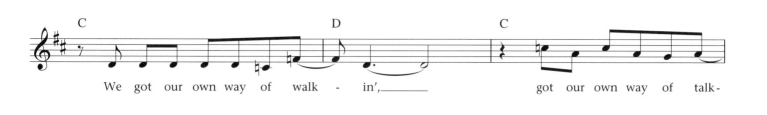

We got our own way of walk-in',_____ got our own way of talk-

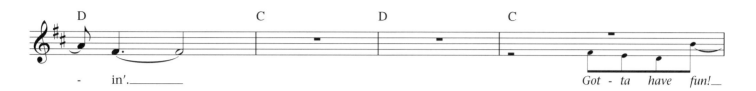

- in'._____   Got - ta have fun!__

__ An - y time__ of the year,__ don't you hear?_____ Got - ta have fun!__

__ Spend-in' cash,__ talk-in' trash.__   Girl, I'll show you a real__

__ good time.__   Come on with me and leave your trou-bles be-hind.__

I__ don't care__ where you've been,__   you ain't been no-where 'til

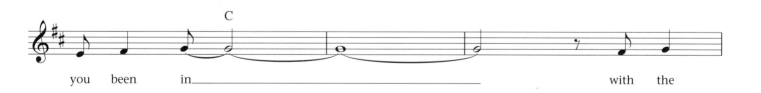

you been in_____   with the

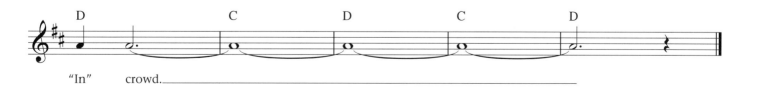

"In" crowd._____

In My Life

In My Room

**Words and Music by
BRIAN WILSON and GARY USHER**

FIRST NOTE

Moderately slow

1. There's a world where I can go and tell my se-crets to,
2. In this world I lock out all my wor-ries and my fears, in my
3. Now it's dark and I'm a-lone, but I won't be a-fraid

room, in my room.

(In my room.)

room. (In my room.)

Do my dream-ing and my schem-ing, lie a-wake and

D.C. al Coda

pray. Do my cry-ing and my sigh-ing, laugh at yes-ter-day.

Coda

room. (In my room, in my room, in my room, in my room, in my room.)

In The Middle Of An Island

Words and Music by
**NICK ACQUAVIVA and
TED VARNICK**

FIRST NOTE

Moderately

In the mid-dle of an is-land in the mid-dle of the o-cean,
is-land, plen-ty time to do some kiss-in',

you and I be-neath the moon-light just the mon-keys and the
plen-ty time for lots of lov-in' walk-ing bare-foot in the

1. palm trees. In the mid-dle of an
2. sand. Though there's no

is-land at all, just a pic-ture on my wall, my dar-ling, how I wish we could

be... in the mid-dle of an is-land in the mid-dle of the o-cean,

you and I for-ev-er, dar-ling in our par-a-dise for two.____

In The Still Of The Nite
(I'll Remember)

Words and Music by
FRED PARRIS

189

It Never Rains (In Southern California)

Words and Music by ALBERT HAMMOND
and MICHAEL HAZELWOOD

190

out of self - re - spect, I'm out - a' bread. I'm un - der -

D.S. to D.S.S.

loved, I'm un - der - fed, I wan - na go home. It nev - er

Isn't She Lovely

Words and Music by STEVIE WONDER

Dm7 G9 C11 F B♭maj7 A7♭9 A7

FIRST NOTE

Moderately fast Shuffle

Is - n't she love - ly, is - n't she won - der - ful?
pret - ty, tru - ly the an - gels' best?
love - ly, life and love are the same.

Is - n't she pre - cious, less than one min - ute old?
Boy, I'm so hap - py, we have been heav - en blessed.
Life is A - i - sha, the mean - ing of her name.

I nev - er thought through love we'd be mak - ing
I can't be - lieve what God has done; through us
Lon - die, it could have not been done with - out

one as love - ly as she. But is - n't she
He's giv - en life to one. But is - n't she
you who con - ceived the one. That's so ver - y

Last time Repeat and Fade

love - ly, made from love?
love - ly, made from love?
love - ly, made from love.

Is - n't she

It Had To Be You

Words by
GUS KAHN

Music by
ISHAM JONES

It had to be you; _____ it had to be you. _____
_____ might nev-er be mean, _____

__ I wan-dered a-round__ and fi-nal-ly found__ the some-bod-y who _____
__ might nev-er be cross__ or try to be boss,__ but they would-n't do. _____

__ could make me be true, _____ could make me be blue, _____ and e-ven be glad

__ just to be sad,__ think-ing of you. _____ Some oth-ers I've seen__

__ For no-bod-y else__ gave me a thrill;__ with all your faults,__ I love you still.

__ It had to be you,__ won-der-ful you,__ had to be you. _____

It Was A Very Good Year

Words and Music by
ERVIN DRAKE

It's A Good Day

**Words and Music by PEGGY LEE
and DAVE BARBOUR**

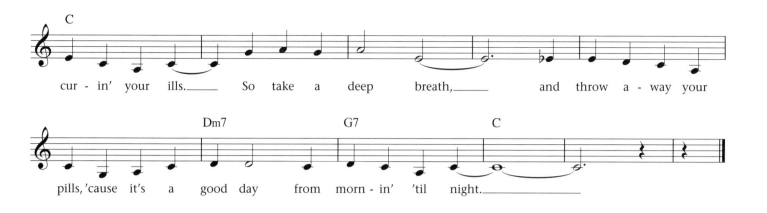

cur - in' your ills.____ So take a deep breath,____ and throw a - way your

pills, 'cause it's a good day from morn - in' 'til night.____

It's A Sin To Tell A Lie

Words and Music by
BILLY MAYHEW

Be sure it's true, when you say, "I love you": it's a

sin to tell a lie.____ Mil - lions of hearts have been

bro - ken, just____ be - cause these words were spo -

ken. I love you, yes, I do, I love you, if you

break my heart, I'll die.____ So be sure it's true, when you

say "I love you": it's a sin to tell a lie!____

It's Now Or Never

Copyright © 1960; Renewed 1988 Gladys Music (ASCAP) and Rachel's Own Music (ASCAP)
All Rights for Gladys Music in the U.S. Administered by Imagem Sounds
All Rights for Rachel's Own Music Administered by A. Schroeder International LLC
Rights for all countries in the world (except U.S.A.) owned by Bideri S.p.A/Gennarelli S.r.l. Administered by A. Schroeder International LLC

It's Too Late

It's Not Unusual

Words and Music by
GORDON MILLS and LES REED

Jamaica Farewell

Words and Music by
IRVING BURGIE

1., 4. Down the way where the nights are gay___ and the sun shines dai - ly on the
2. Sounds of laugh - ter ev - 'ry - where___ and the danc - ing girls sway - ing
3. Down at the mar - ket you can hear___ la - dies cry out while on their

moun - tain top,___ I took a trip on a sail - ing ship___ and when I
to and fro,___ I must de - clare___ my heart is there,___ though I've
heads they bear___ ac - kie, rice; salt fish are nice,___ and the

reached Ja - mai - ca, I made a stop.___ But I'm sad to say I'm
been from Maine___ to Mex - i - co.___
rum is fine___ an - y time of year.___

on my way.___ Won't be back for man - y a day.___ My heart is down,___ my head is

turn - ing a - round,___ I had to leave a lit - tle girl in King - ston town.___

Java Jive

Words and Music by
MILTON DRAKE and
BEN OAKLAND

jiv - in' and me,___ a cup, a cup, a cup, a cup, a cup.

Bos - ton bean,___ soy bean,___ li - ma bean,___ string bean.___

I'm not keen___ for a bean___ un - less it is a cheer - y cof - fee bean:

D.C. al Coda

Coda

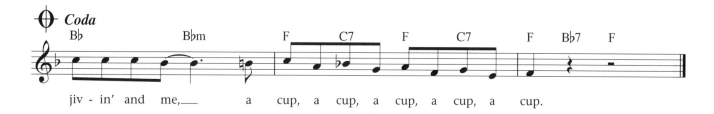

jiv - in' and me,___ a cup, a cup, a cup, a cup, a cup.

Kansas City

Words and Music by
JERRY LEIBER and MIKE STOLLER

Kisses Sweeter Than Wine

Words by RONNIE GILBERT, LEE HAYS, FRED HELLERMAN and PETE SEEGER

Music by
HUDDIE LEDBETTER

Additional Lyrics

3. I worked mighty hard and so did my wife,
a-workin' hand in hand to make a good life.
With corn in the fields and wheat in the bins,
and then, oh, Lord, I was the father of twins.
Chorus

4. Our children numbered just about four,
and they all had sweethearts knock on the door.
They all got married, and they didn't wait.
I was, oh, Lord, the grandfather of eight.
Chorus

5. Now we are old and ready to go.
We get to thinkin' what happened a long time ago.
We had lots of kids and trouble and pain,
but, oh, Lord, we'd do it again.
Chorus

Knock Three Times

Words and Music by IRWIN LEVINE
and LARRY RUSSELL BROWN

La Vie En Rose
(Take Me To Your Heart Again)

Original French Lyrics by EDITH PIAF
English Lyrics by MACK DAVID

Music by
LOUIS GUGLIELMI

Lyrics:

Hold me close and hold me fast, the mag-ic spell you cast, this is la vie en rose.

When you kiss me heav-en sighs, and though I close my eyes I see la vie en rose.

When you press me to your heart, I'm in a world a-part, a world where ros-es bloom. And when you speak, an-gels sing from a-bove; ev-'ry-day words seem to turn in-to love songs.

Give your heart and soul to me, and life will al-ways be la vie en rose.

The Lady Is A Tramp

Words by
LORENZ HART

Music by
RICHARD RODGERS

The Last Time

Words and Music by
MICK JAGGER and KEITH RICHARDS

Lay Down Sally

Words and Music by ERIC CLAPTON,
MARCY LEVY and GEORGE TERRY

Lazy Day

Words by
TONY POWERS

Music by
GEORGE FISCHOFF

Leap For A Man, Girls, It's Leap Year

Words and Music by HARRY PEASE,
ED G. NELSON and GILBERT DODGE

Lazy River

Words and Music by
HOAGY CARMICHAEL
and SIDNEY ARODIN

Lazybones

Words and Music by
HOAGY CARMICHAEL
and JOHNNY MERCER

Lean On Me

Words and Music by
BILL WITHERS

D.S. al Coda

Coda

Leaning On A Lamp Post

Words and Music by
NOEL GAY

Fine   D.S. al Coda

by. (Doo-wack-a, doo-wack-a, doo-wack-a, doo-wack-a, doo-wack-a, doo-wack-a, doo.)   She

⊕ Coda

She's not the kind of girl to be late for,_____ but

this one I'd break an-y date for._____ I won't have to ask what she's

D.S.S. al Fine

late for,_____ she'd nev-er leave me flat, she's not a girl like that. She's

Loving You

Words and Music by
JERRY LEIBER and MIKE STOLLER

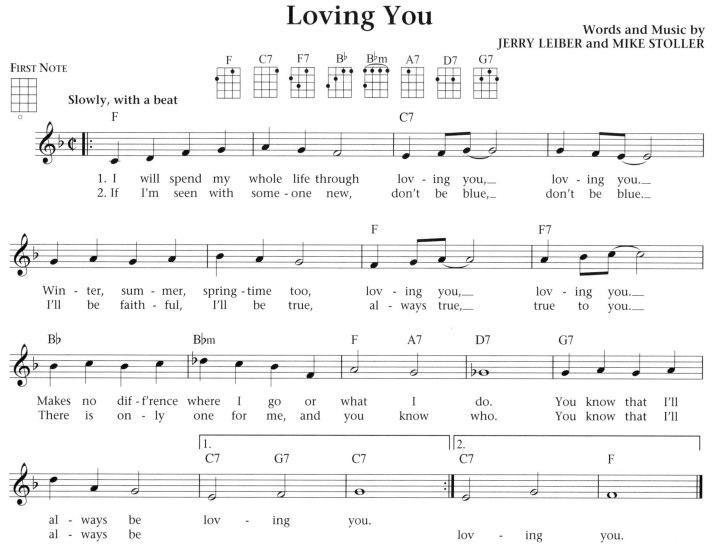

FIRST NOTE

Slowly, with a beat

1. I will spend my whole life through   lov-ing you,_   lov-ing you._
2. If I'm seen with some-one new,   don't be blue,_   don't be blue._

Win-ter, sum-mer, spring-time too,   lov-ing you,_   lov-ing you._
I'll be faith-ful, I'll be true,   al-ways true,_   true to you._

Makes no dif-f'rence where I go or what I do.   You know that I'll
There is on-ly one for me, and you know who.   You know that I'll

1.
al-ways be lov-ing you.

2.
al-ways be   lov-ing you.

217

Leaving On A Jet Plane

Words and Music by
JOHN DENVER

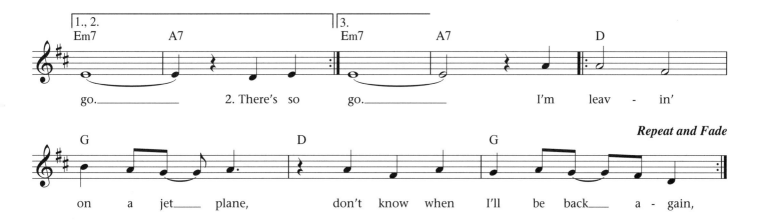

Let A Smile Be Your Umbrella

Words by IRVING KAHAL
and FRANCIS WHEELER

Music by
SAMMY FAIN

Lemon Tree

Words and Music by
WILL HOLT

Let's Get Away From It All

**Words and Music by
TOM ADAIR and
MATT DENNIS**

Let Your Love Flow

Words and Music by
LARRY E. WILLIAMS

Longing To Belong

Written by
EDDIE VEDDER

The Look Of Love

Words by
HAL DAVID

Music by
BURT BACHARACH

Lookin' For Love

Words and Music by WANDA MALLETTE,
PATTI RYAN and BOB MORRISON

Lookin' Out My Back Door

Words and Music
JOHN FOGERTY

Love And Marriage

Words by
SAMMY CAHN

Music by
JAMES VAN HEUSEN

L-O-V-E

Words and Music by
BERT KAEMPFERT
and MILT GABLER

Love Is Just Around The Corner

Words and Music by LEO ROBIN
and LEWIS E. GENSLER

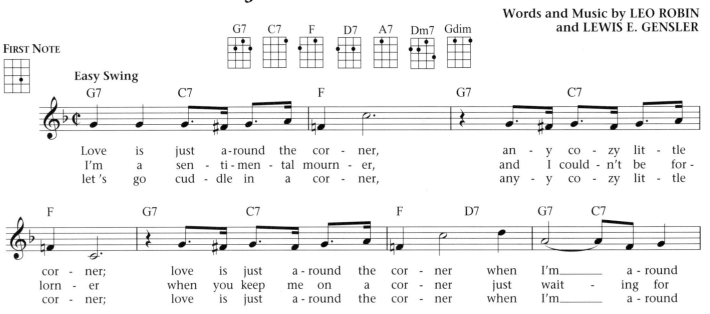

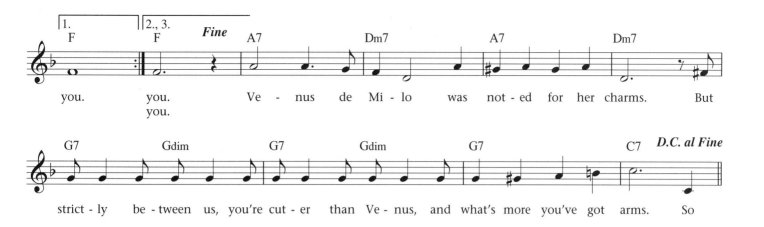

you. you. Ve - nus de Mi - lo was not - ed for her charms. But
you.

strict - ly be - tween us, you're cut - er than Ve - nus, and what's more you've got arms. So

Lulu's Back In Town

Words by
AL DUBIN

Music by
HARRY WARREN

FIRST NOTE

Moderato with a swing

Got - ta get my old tux - e - do pressed,__ got - ta sew a but - ton
Got - ta get a half - a - buck some - where,__ got - ta shine my shoes and
You can tell the mail - man not to call, ___ I ain't com - in' home un -

on my vest;__ 'cause to - night I've got - a look my best,__
slick my hair;__ got - ta get my - self a bou - ton - nière,__
til the fall.___ And I might not get back home at all,__

Lu - lu's back in town.___ Lu - lu's back in town.___ You can

tell all my pets,__ all my Har - lem co - quettes,__ Mis - ter

O - tis re - grets that he won't be a - roun'.__

Love Is In The Air

Words and Music by HARRY VANDA
and GEORGE YOUNG

The Magic Islands

**Lyrics and Adaptation by
KEN DARBY**

**Traditional Polynesian Melody
"Ku'u Lei Awapuhi"**

Far a-way the mag-ic is - lands call to me a-cross the
Far a-way the mag-ic is - lands call to me a-cross the

sea,_____ and the mag-ic of the is - lands
years,_____ and the mag-ic of the is - lands

thrills my heart with mem-o - ry._____
fills my lone-ly dreams with tears._____ White gin-ger was in bloom,_____

_ it filled the air_____ with sweet per-fume and we were there._____

_ Two shad-ows on the sand,_____ a tro-pic moon a - bove_____

1.
_ and we were lost, so lost in love._____

2.
love._____

© 1956 (Renewed 2002) Flea Market Music, Inc.

MacArthur Park

Words and Music by
JIMMY WEBB

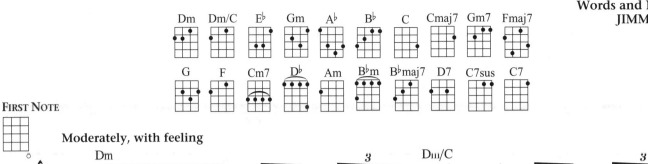

FIRST NOTE

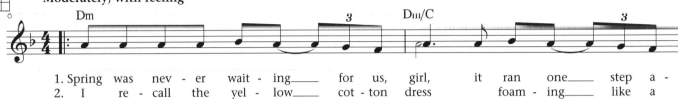

Moderately, with feeling

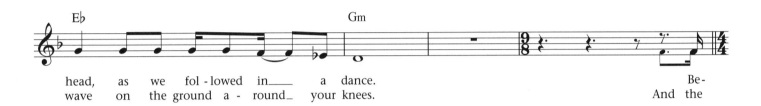

1. Spring was nev - er wait - ing___ for us, girl, it ran one___ step a -
2. I re - call the yel - low___ cot - ton dress foam - ing___ like a

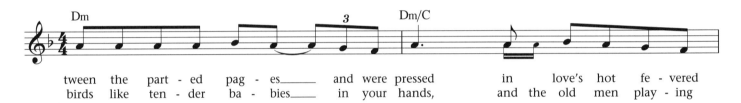

head, as we fol - lowed in___ a dance. Be -
wave on the ground a - round___ your knees. And the

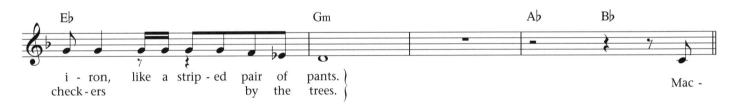

tween the part - ed pag - es___ and were pressed in love's hot fe - vered
birds like ten - der ba - bies___ in your hands, and the old men play - ing

i - ron, like a strip - ed pair of pants. Mac -
check - ers by the trees.

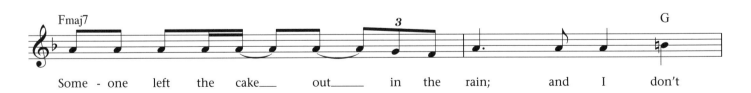

Ar - thur Park is melt - ing in the dark, all the sweet, green ic - ing flow - ing down.

Some - one left the cake___ out___ in the rain; and I don't

think that I___ can take it, 'cause it took so long to bake___ it, and I'll

Make Your Own Kind Of Music

Words and Music by BARRY MANN
and CYNTHIA WEIL

Mama Tried

Words and Music by
MERLE HAGGARD

Mame

Music and Lyric by
JERRY HERMAN

Memories Are Made Of This

Words and Music by RICHARD DEHR,
FRANK MILLER and TERRY GILKYSON

Mammas Don't Let Your Babies
Grow Up To Be Cowboys

Words and Music by
ED BRUCE and PATSY BRUCE

Mam-mas don't let your ba-bies grow up to be cow-boys,

Don't let 'em pick gui-tars and drive them old trucks; let 'em be doc-tors and

law-yers, and such. Mam-mas___ don't let your ba-bies grow up___ to be

cow-boys. They'll nev-er stay___ home, and they're al-ways a-lone,

e-ven with some-one___ they love.

1. Cow-boys ain't eas-y to
2. Cow-boys like smok-y ole

love, and they're hard-er___ to hold.
pool rooms and clear moun-tain morn-ings.

They'd rath-er
Lit-tle warm

give you a song than dia-monds and gold.
pup-pies and chil-dren and girls of the night.

Rock-star belt
Them that don't

buck-les and old fad-ed Le-vi's and each night be-gins a new day.
know him won't like him and them that do some-times won't know how to take him.

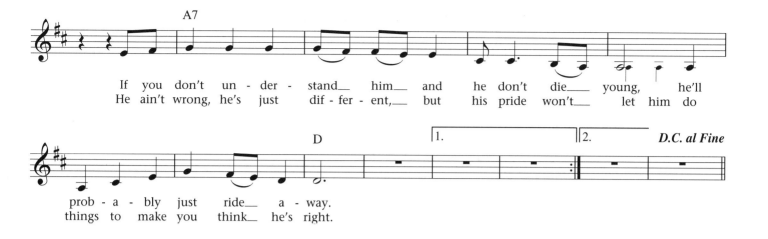

If you don't un-der-stand__ him__ and he don't die__ young, he'll
He ain't wrong, he's just dif-fer-ent,__ but his pride won't__ let him do

prob-a-bly just ride__ a-way.
things to make you think__ he's right.

More
(Ti Guarderó Nel Cuore)

Italian lyrics by MARCELLO CIORCIOLINI
English lyrics by NORMAN NEWELL

Music by NINO OLIVIERO
and RIZ ORTOLANI

More than the great-est love the world has known; this is the
More than the sim-ple words I try to say; I on-ly

love I'll give to you a-lone.
live to love you more each day. More than you'll

ev-er know, my arms long to hold you so, my life will be in your keep-ing,

wak-ing, sleep-ing, laugh-ing, weep-ing. Long-er than al-ways is a long, long time;

but far be-yond for-ev-er you'll be mine. I know I nev-er lived be-

fore and my heart is ver-y sure no one else could love you more.__

A Man And A Woman
(Un Homme Et Une Femme)

Original Words by PIERRE BAROUH
English Words by JERRY KELLER

Music by
FRANCIS LAI

Bbmaj7
wait - ing for us there, call - ing for us there____ that on - ly lov - ing____
chance that in the light, in to - mor - row's light____ they'll be to - geth - er____

Em7

A7 **Dmaj7** **N.C.** **Dmaj7** **Em7**

1.
____ can give the heart. When life is love,____ to - geth - er____
2.
____ so much in

A7 **Dmaj7** **Em7**
____ so much in love.____ So, tell me____ you're not a -

Dmaj7 **Dbmaj7** **Cmaj7**
fraid to take the chance, real - ly take a chance. Let your heart be - gin to dance,
mu - sic of a glance, of a fleet - ing glance to the mu - sic of ro - mance,

1. **Dbmaj7** 2. **Cmaj7** **Dbmaj7** **Dmaj7**
let it sing and dance, to the
of a new ro - mance, take a chance.

Maneater

Words by SARA ALLEN, DARYL HALL
and JOHN OATES

Music by DARYL HALL
and JOHN OATES

- eat - er. Oh,__ here she comes,__ watch out boy,__ she'll chew you up.____

Oh,__ here she comes,__ she's a man - eat - er. 2. I

Massachusetts (The Lights Went Out In)

Words and Music by BARRY GIBB,
ROBIN GIBB and MAURICE GIBB

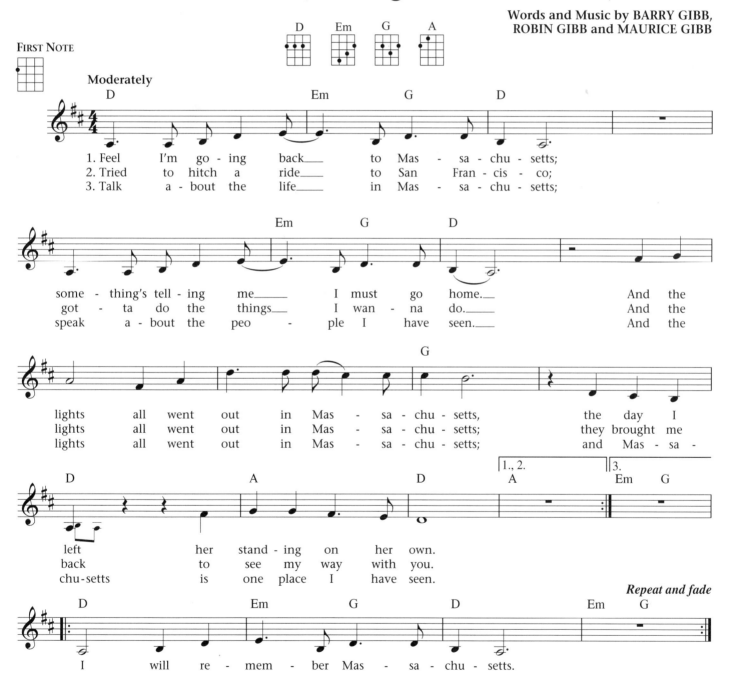

1. Feel I'm go - ing back____ to Mas - sa - chu - setts;
2. Tried to hitch a ride____ to San Fran - cis - co;
3. Talk a - bout the life____ in Mas - sa - chu - setts;

some - thing's tell - ing me____ I must go home.__ And the
got - ta do the things____ I wan - na do.__ And the
speak a - bout the peo - ple I have seen.____ And the

lights all went out in Mas - sa - chu - setts, the day I
lights all went out in Mas - sa - chu - setts; they brought me
lights all went out in Mas - sa - chu - setts; and Mas - sa -

left her stand - ing on her own.
back to see my way with you.
chu-setts is one place I have seen.

Repeat and fade

I will re - mem - ber Mas - sa - chu - setts.

Mr. Bojangles

Words and Music by
JERRY JEFF WALKER

Additional Lyrics

2. I met him in a cell in New Orleans;
   I was down and out.
   He looked to me to be the eyes of age,
   as he spoke right out.
   He talked of life, talked of life,
   laughed, slapped his leg a step.

3. He said his name, Bojangles, and he
   danced a lick across the cell.
   He grabbed his pants for a better stance,
   then he jumped so high and clicked his heels.
   He let go a laugh, let go a laugh,
   shook back his clothes all around.
   Chorus

4. He danced for those at minstrel shows
   and county fairs throughout the South.
   He spoke through tears of fifteen years
   how his dog and him traveled about.
   The dog up and died, he up and died,
   after twenty years he still grieves.

5. He said "I dance now at every chance in honky tonks
   for drinks and tips.
   But most the time I spend behind these county bars
   because I drinks a bit."
   He shook his head, and as he shook his head
   I heard someone ask, "Please."
   Chorus

Mr. Tambourine Man

Words and Music by
BOB DYLAN

FIRST NOTE

Moderately

Additional Lyrics

2. Take me on a trip upon your magic swirlin' ship.
My senses have been stripped,
my hands can't feel to grip;
my toes too numb to step, wait only for my boot heels
to be wanderin'.
I'm ready to go anywhere, I'm ready for to fade
into my own parade; cast your dancin' spell my way.
I promise to go under it.
Chorus

3. Though you might hear laughin' spinnin',
swingin' madly across the sun;
it's not aimed at anyone, it's just escapin' on the run.
And, but for the sky there are no fences facin'.
And if you hear vague traces of skippin' reels of rhyme
to your tambourine in time, it's just a ragged clown behind;
I wouldn't pay it any mind. It's just a shadow you're
seein' that he's chasin'.
Chorus

4. Then take me disappearin' through the smoke rings of my mind,
down the foggy ruins of time, far past the frozen leaves;
the haunted, frightened trees out to the windy beach
far from the twisted reach of crazy sorrow.
Yes, to dance beneath the diamond sky with one hand wavin' free,
silhouetted by the sea; circled by the circus sands.
With all memory and fate driven deep beneath the waves,
let me forget about today until tomorrow.
Chorus

Mockin' Bird Hill

Words and Music by
VAUGHN HORTON

Mrs. Brown You've Got A Lovely Daughter

Words and Music by
TREVOR PEACOCK

Monday, Monday

Words and Music by
JOHN PHILLIPS

-day,   can't trust that day.   Mon - day, Mon - day,

it just turns out that way.   Mon - day, Mon - day,   won't go a - way.

Mon - day, Mon - day,   it's here to stay.

Moonglow

**Words and Music by WILL HUDSON,
EDDIE DE LANGE and IRVING MILLS**

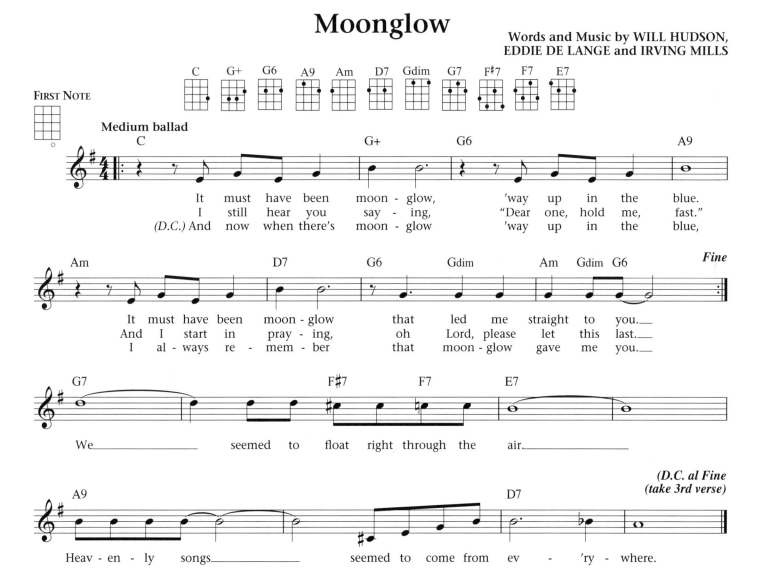

FIRST NOTE

Medium ballad

C   **G+**   **G6**   **A9**

It must have been moon - glow,   'way up in the blue.
I still hear you say - ing,   "Dear one, hold me, fast."
(D.C.) And now when there's moon - glow   'way up in the blue,

Am   **D7**   **G6**   **Gdim**   **Am**   **Gdim**   **G6**   *Fine*

It must have been moon - glow   that led me straight to you.
And I start in pray - ing,   oh Lord, please let this last.
I al - ways re - mem - ber   that moon - glow gave me you.

G7   **F#7**   **F7**   **E7**

We   seemed to float right through the air.

*(D.C. al Fine
(take 3rd verse)*

A9   **D7**

Heav - en - ly songs   seemed to come from ev - 'ry - where.

Moon Shadow

Words and Music by
YUSUF ISLAM

253

Moondance

Words and Music by
VAN MORRISON

moon - dance_ with_ you,_ my love?_ Can I_

just make_ some_ more_ ro - mance_ with_ you,_ my love?_

1., 2. | **3.**

_ 2. Well, I | _ One more moon - dance with you in the moon-light
3. It's a

on a mag - ic night. La la_ la_ la, in the

moon - light on a mag - ic night. Can't

I_ just have_ one more_ moon - dance_ with you, my_ love?_

More Today Than Yesterday

Words and Music by
PAT UPTON

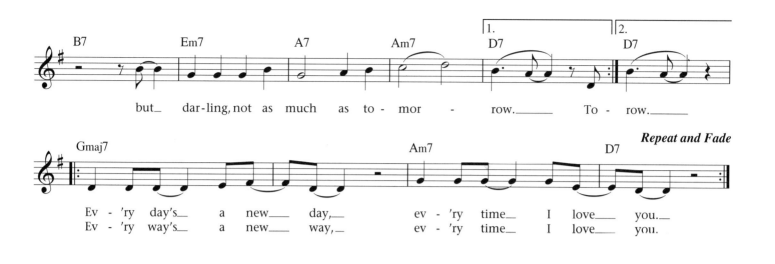

but__ dar-ling, not as much as to-mor — row.__ To - row.__

Repeat and Fade

Ev - 'ry day's__ a new__ day,__ ev - 'ry time__ I love__ you.__
Ev - 'ry way's__ a new__ way,__ ev - 'ry time__ I love__ you.

Morning Has Broken

Words by
ELEANOR FARJEON

Music by
YUSUF ISLAM

FIRST NOTE

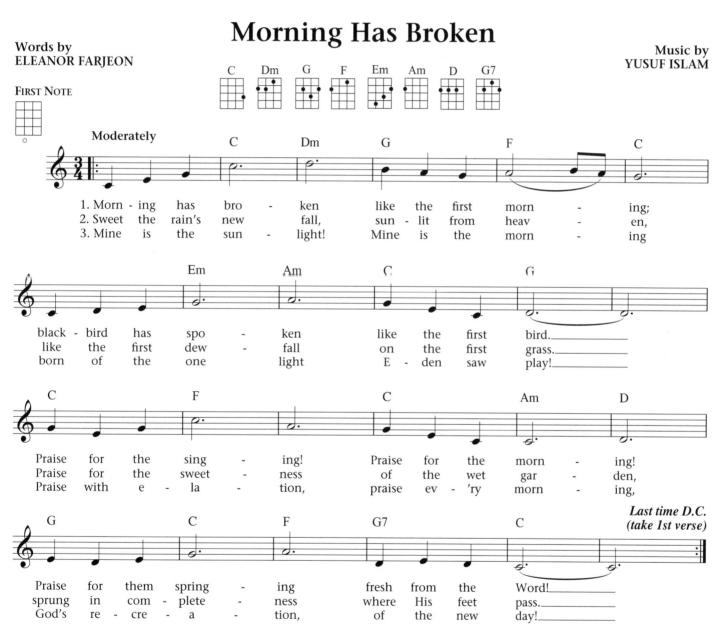

1. Morn - ing has bro - ken like the first morn - ing;
2. Sweet the rain's new fall, sun - lit from heav - en,
3. Mine is the sun - light! Mine is the morn - ing

black - bird has spo - ken like the first bird.__
like the first dew - fall on the first grass.__
born of the one light E - den saw play!__

Praise for the sing - ing! Praise for the morn - ing!
Praise for the sweet - ness of the wet gar - den,
Praise with e - la - tion, praise ev - 'ry morn - ing,

Last time D.C.
(take 1st verse)

Praise for them spring - ing fresh from the Word!__
sprung in com - plete - ness where His feet pass.__
God's re - cre - a - tion, of the new day!__

Move It On Over

Words and Music by
HANK WILLIAMS

With spirit

1. Came in last night at half-past-ten,___ that baby of mine would-n't
(2.) dog-house here is might-y small,___ but it's bet-ter than no
3. *See additional lyrics*

let me in.___ So, move it on o-ver, *(move it on o-ver)*
house at all.___ So, ease it on o-ver, *(move it on o-ver)*

move it on o-ver. *(Move it on o-ver.)* Move o-ver li'l dog, 'cause the
drag it on o-ver. *(Move it on o-ver.)* Move o-ver old dog, 'cause a

big dog's mov-in'___ in.___ She's changed the lock on our front door,___ now
new dog's mov-in'___ in.___ She told me not to play a-round,_ but

my door key don't fit no more._ So, get it on o-ver, *(move it on o-ver)*
I done let the deal go down._ So, pack it on o-ver, *(move it on o-ver)*

scoot it on o-ver. *(Move it on o-ver.)* Move o-ver skin-ny dog, 'cause the
tote it on o-ver. *(Move it on o-ver.)* Move o-ver nice dog, 'cause a

1.-4.
fat dog's mov-in'___ in.___ 2. This
mad dog's mov-in'___

5.
in.___

Additional Lyrics

3. She warned me once, she warned me twice,
but I don't take no one's advice.
So scratch it on over, *(move it on over,)*
shake it on over. *(Move it on over.)*
Move over short dog, 'cause a tall dog's movin' in.

4. She'll crawl back to me, on her knees,
I'll be busy scratchin' fleas.
So slide it on over, *(move it on over,)*
sneak it on over. *(Move it on over.)*
Move over good dog, 'cause a bad dog's movin' in.

5. Remember, pup, before you whine,
that side's yours and this side's mine.
So shove it on over, *(move it on over,)*
sweep it on over. *(Move it on over.)*
Move over cold dog, 'cause a hot dog's movin' in.

The M.T.A.

Words and Music by
JACQUELINE STEINER
and BESS HAWES

Music To Watch Girls By

By SID RAMIN

My Cup Runneth Over

Words by
TOM JONES

Music by
HARVEY SCHMIDT

My Way

English Words by PAUL ANKA
Original French Words by GILLES THIBAULT

Music by JACQUES REVAUX
and CLAUDE FRANCOIS

Never On Sunday

Words by
BILLY TOWNE

Music by
MANOS HADJIDAKIS

1. Oh, you can kiss me on a Mon-day, a Mon-day, a Mon-day is ver-y, ver-y
2. cool day, a hot day, a wet day, which ev-er one you

good. Or you can kiss me on a Tues-day, a Tues-day, a Tues-day, in fact I wish you
choose. Or try to kiss me on a gray day, a May day, a pay day, and see if I re-

would. Or you can kiss me on a Wednes-day, a Thurs-day, a
fuse. And if you make it on a bleak day, a freak day, a

Fri-day and Sat-ur-day is best. But nev-er, nev-er on a
week-day, why you can be my guest. But nev-er, nev-er on a

Sun-day, a Sun-day, a Sun-day, 'cause that's my day of rest. Come an-y
Sun-day, a Sun-day, the one day I need a lit-tle rest.

day_____ and you'll be my guest,_____ an-y day you say,_____ but my day of

rest. Just name the day_____ that you like the best,_____ on-ly stay a-

way_____ on my day of rest. 2. Oh, you can kiss me on a

No Moon At All

By DAVE MANN
and REDD EVANS

No Particular Place to Go

Words and Music by
CHUCK BERRY

C   F   G7

FIRST NOTE

With a beat

Rid-ing a-long in my au-to-mo- bile.   My ba - by be-side me at the
bile,   I was anx - ious to tell her the way I
go,   so we parked way out on the Ko - ko-
boose,   still try - ing to get her belt un-

wheel: I stole a kiss at the turn of a mile,
feel: So I told her soft - ly and___ sin - cere,
mo.   The night was young and the moon___ was gold,
loose,   all the way home I held___ a grudge,

my cu - ri - os - i - ty run - ning wild.
and she leaned and whis - pered in my ear.
so we both de - cid - ed to take a stroll.
for the safe - ty belt___ that would - n't budge.

Cruis-ing and play-ing the ra - di - o   with no par - tic - u - lar place to
Cud - dling more_ and driv - ing slow   with no par - tic - u - lar place to
Can you im - ag - ine the way I felt?   I couldn't un - fast - en her safe - ty
Cruis-ing and play-ing the ra - di - o   with no par - tic - u - lar place to

1.-3.   N.C.   4.

go.   Rid - ing a - long in my au - to - mo-   go.___
go.   No___ par - tic - u - lar place_ to
belt.   Rid - ing a - long in my cal - a -

Nowhere Man

Word and Music by JOHN LENNON
and PAUL McCARTNEY

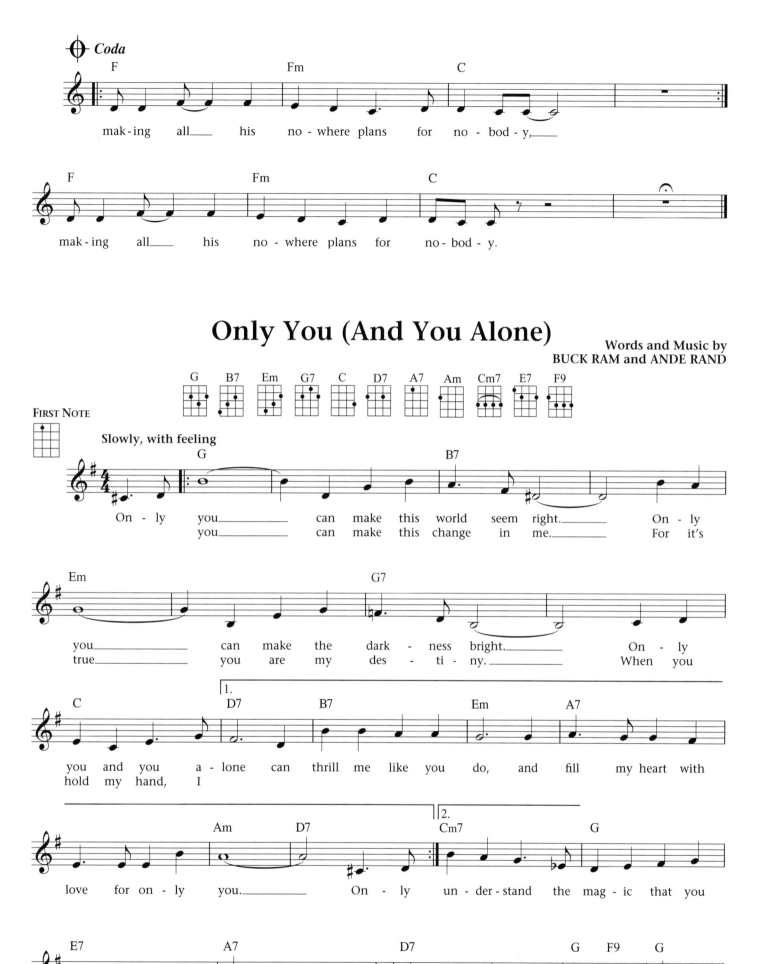

Octopus's Garden

Words and Music by
RICHARD STARKEY

Oh, what joy___ for ev-'ry girl and boy___ know-ing___ they're

hap-py and they're safe. We would be so hap-py___ you and me,___

___ no one there to tell us what to do.___ I'd like to be___

1.

un-der the sea___ in an oct-o-pus-'s gar-den with you.___ in an

2.

___ In an oct-o-pus-'s gar-den with you.

Old Cape Cod

Words and Music by
CLAIRE ROTHROCK, MILT YAKUS
and ALLEN JEFFREY

If you're fond of sand dunes and salt y air,____
If you like the taste of a lob - ster stew,____
If you spend an eve - ning, you'll want to stay____

quaint lit - tle vil - lag - es here and there;____
served by a win - dow with an o - cean view;____
watch - ing the moon - light on Cape Cod Bay.____

you're sure to fall in love with old Cape Cod.____

old Cape Cod.____ Wind - ing roads that seem to beck - on you,

miles of green be - neath the skies of blue; church bells chim - ing on a

D.C. al Fine
(take 2nd ending)

Sun - day morn' re - mind you of the town where you were born.

On A Carousel

Words and Music by
TONY HICKS, GRAHAM NASH
and ALLAN CLARKE

One Love

Words and Music by
BOB MARLEY

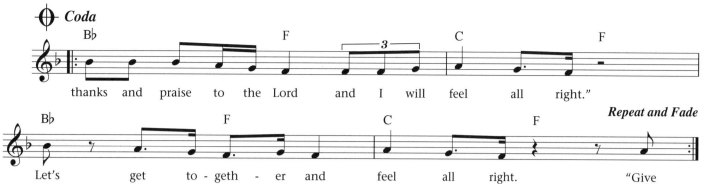

Coda Bb   F   3   C   F

thanks and praise to the Lord and I will feel all right."

Repeat and Fade

Bb   F   C   F

Let's get to-geth-er and feel all right. "Give

One Fine Day

Words and Music by GERRY GOFFIN
and CAROLE KING

FIRST NOTE

F C Dm Bbm Bb C7 F7 Cm7 Dm7 G7

Briskly

One___ fine day,___ you'll look at me,
The arms I long for___ will o-pen wide,___
One___ fine day,___ we'll meet once more,___

and you will know___ our love was meant___ to be.___
and you'll be proud___ to have me right by your side.___
and then you'll want___ the love you threw a-way be-fore.___

To Coda   1.   2nd & 3rd x

One_ fine day___ you're gon-na want me for your girl.

2. girl.

Though_ I know you're_ the kind_ of boy___ who on-ly wants to run a-round.___

I'll_ keep wait-ing,_ and some-day, dar-ling,_ you'll come to

D.C. al Coda   *Coda*

me when you_ want to set-tle down, oh.   girl.___

The Open Road

Words and Music by
JIM BELOFF

no wait-ing lines,_____ just West-ern pines_____ all_ a - round._____

Give me the o - pen road,_____ the o - pen road

is where I'm bound. I guess I've got to roam, 'cause the o - pen

road will lead me home._____

Our Day Will Come

**Words by
BOB HILLIARD**

**Music by
MORT GARSON**

FIRST NOTE

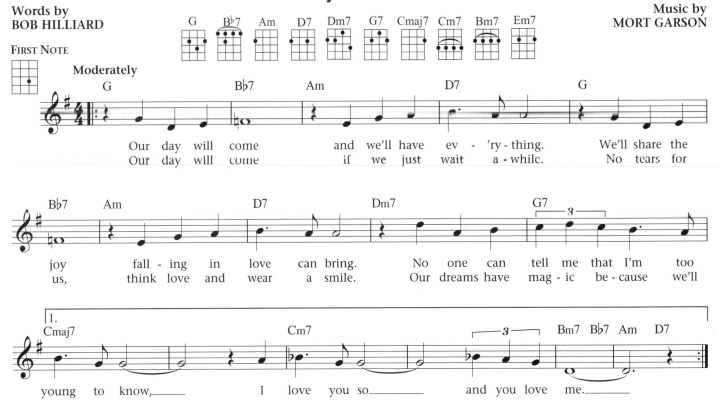

Our day will come and we'll have ev-'ry-thing.
Our day will come if we just wait a-while.

We'll share the
No tears for

joy, fall-ing in love can bring. No one can tell me that I'm too
us, think love and wear a smile. Our dreams have mag-ic be-cause we'll

1.
young to know,___ I love you so___ and you love me.___

2.
al-ways stay in love this way, our day___ will come.___

Paddlin' Madelin' Home

Words and Music by
HARRY WOODS

Peaceful Easy Feeling

Words and Music by
JACK TEMPCHIN

Additional Lyrics

2. And I found out a long time ago
what a woman can do to your soul.
Ah, but she can't take you anyway,
you don't already know how to go.
Chorus

3. I get this feelin' I may know you
as a lover and a friend.
But this voice keeps whispering in my other ear,
tells me I may never see you again.
Chorus

P.S. I Love You

Words and Music by JOHN LENNON
and PAUL McCARTNEY

People Got To Be Free

Words and Music by FELIX CAVALIERE
and EDWARD BRIGATI, JR.

Am ... Em ... F

eas - y, eas - y thing it should be._____ Why can't you and me__
solve it in - di - vid - u - al - ly,_____ And I'll do un - to you__

C ... G7 N.C. ... G7 N.C.

__ learn to love one an - oth - er? me.
__ what you do__ to

F ... C ... G7sus ... C

They'll be shout - in' from the moun - tain on out to the sea,_____
Oh,_____ what a feel - in' just come o - ver me;__ it's e -

F ... C ... G7sus ... C

no two ways a - bout it, peo - ple have to be free._____
nough to move a moun - tain, make a blind__ man see._____

F ... C ... G7sus ... C

Ask me my o - pin - ion, my o - pin - ion will be,_____ it's a
Ev - 'ry - bod - y's danc - in', come on let's__ go see;_____ there's

F ... C ... G7sus ... C C7

nat - 'ral sit - u - a - tion for a man to be free._____
peace__ in the val - ley, now we all can be free._____

G7 ... C C7 G7 ... C C7 G7

Repeat and Fade

C C7 G7 ... C C7 G7 ... C C7 G7

Spoken: Look, see that train over there? Now that's the train of freedom, it's about to arrive any minute now.
You know it's been long over - due, look out 'cause it's comin' right on through. Oh, happy day!

Please Mr. Postman

Words and Music by ROBERT BATEMAN,
GEORGIA DOBBINS, WILLIAM GARRETT,
FREDDIE GORMAN and BRIAN HOLLAND

Puff, The Magic Dragon

Words and Music by LENNIE LIPTON
and PETER YARROW

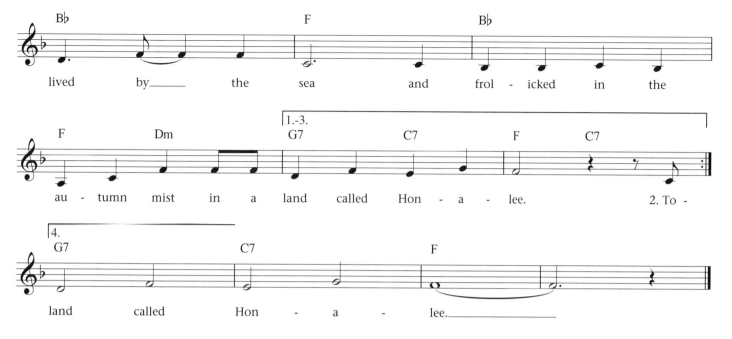

lived   by____   the   sea   and   frol - icked   in   the

1.-3.

au - tumn   mist   in   a   land   called   Hon - a - lee.   2. To -

4.

land   called   Hon - a - lee.____

Additional Lyrics

2. Together they would travel on a boat with billowed sail.
   Jackie kept a lookout perched on Puff's gigantic tail.
   Noble kings and princes would bow when e'er they came.
   Pirate ships would low'r their flags when Puff roared out his name. Oh!
   Chorus

3. A dragon lives forever, but not so little boys.
   Painted wings and giant rings make way for other toys.
   One gray night it happened, Jackie Paper came no more,
   and Puff that mighty dragon, he ceased his fearless roar.
   Chorus

4. His head was bent in sorrow, green tears fell like rain.
   Puff no longer went to play along the Cherry Lane.
   Without his lifelong friend, Puff could not be brave,
   so Puff that mighty dragon sadly slipped into his cave. Oh!
   Chorus

Ram On

Words and Music by
PAUL McCARTNEY

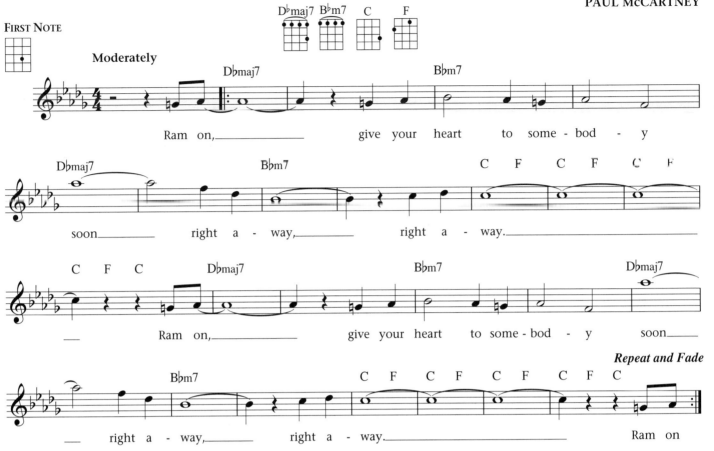

Ram on, give your heart to some-bod-y soon right a-way, right a-way.

Ram on, give your heart to some-bod-y soon right a-way, right a-way. Ram on

Ramblin' Rose

Words and Music by
NOEL SHERMAN and JOE SHERMAN

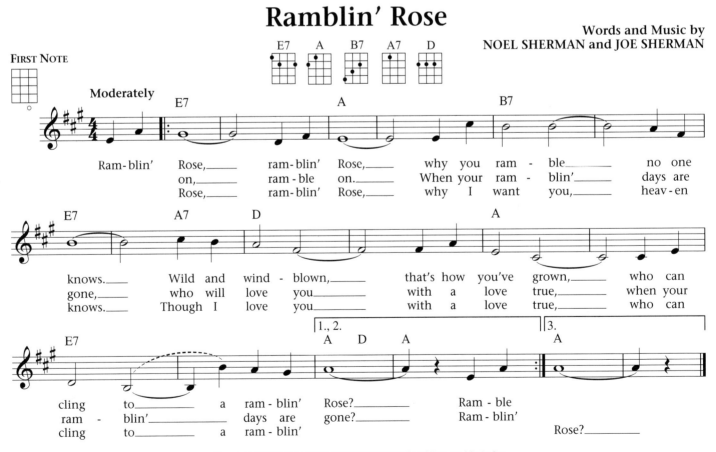

Ram-blin' Rose, ram-blin' Rose, why you ram-ble no one
on, ram-ble on. When your ram-blin' days are
Rose, ram-blin' Rose, why I want you, heav-en

knows. Wild and wind-blown, that's how you've grown, who can
gone, who will love you with a love true, when your
knows. Though I love you with a love true, who can

cling to a ram-blin' Rose? Ram-ble
ram-blin' days are gone? Ram-blin'
cling to a ram-blin' Rose?

Ramblin' Man

Words and Music by
DICKEY BETTS

Red Roses For A Blue Lady

Words and Music by SID TEPPER
and ROY C. BENNETT

I want some red ros-es for a blue la-dy. Mis-ter Flo-rist,
red ros-es for a blue la-dy. Send them to the

take my or-der, please._____ We had a sil-ly quar-rel the oth-er day.__
sweet-est gal in town._____ And if they do the

Hope these pret-ty flow-ers chase her blues a-way.___ Wrap up some

trick, I'll hur-ry back to pick your best white or-chid for her wed-ding gown._____

Red Sails In The Sunset

Words by
JIMMY KENNEDY

Music by
HUGH WILLIAMS (WILL GROSZ)

1. Red sails in the sun-set way out on the sea.
2. He sailed at the dawn-ing, all day I've been blue.

Oh, car-ry my loved one home safe-ly to me.
Red sails in the sun-set, I'm trust-ing in you.

Swift wings you must bor-row, make straight for the shore.

We mar-ry to-mor-row and he goes sail-ing no more.

Release Me

FIRST NOTE

Words and Music by ROBERT YOUNT,
EDDIE MILLER and DUB WILLIAMS

Please re - lease me, let me go, for I don't
I have found a new love, dear, and I will
Please re - lease me, can't you see you'd be a

love you an - y - more. To waste our lives would be a sin.
al - ways want her near. Her lips are warm while yours are cold.
fool to cling to me. To live a lie would bring us pain.

1., 2.
Re - lease me and let me love a - gain.
Re - lease me, my dar - ling, let me go.
So re - lease me and let me love a - **3.** gain.

Roll In My Sweet Baby's Arms

FIRST NOTE

Traditional

1. Ain't gon - na work on the rail - road. Ain't gon - na
Chorus: Roll in my sweet ba - by's arms, roll in my

work on the farm. Gon - na lay 'round the shack 'til the
sweet ba - by's arms.

mail train gets back and I'll roll in my sweet ba - by's arms.

Additional Lyrics

2. Now where was you last Saturday night, while I was lyin' in jail?
   Walkin' the streets with another man, you wouldn't even go my bail.
   Chorus

3. I know your parents don't like me; they drove me away from your door.
   If I had my life to live over again, I'd never go there anymore.
   Chorus

4. Mama's a beauty operator, sister can weave and can spin.
   Dad's got an interest in the old cotton mill, just watch the money roll in.
   Chorus

289

Return To Sender

Words and Music by OTIS BLACKWELL
and WINFIELD SCOTT

Rockin' Robin

Words and Music by
J. THOMAS

1. He rocks in the tree-top all the day long, hop-pin' and a-bop-pin' and a
2. Ev-'ry lit-tle swal-low, ev-'ry chick-a-dee, ev-'ry lit-tle bird in the

sing-in' his song. All the lit-tle birds on Jay-bird Street,
tall oak tree. The wise old owl, the big black crow,

love to hear the rob-in go "Tweet, tweet, tweet." } Rock-in' Rob-in,___
flap their wings, sing-in' "Go bird, go."

Rock-in' Rob-in, blow, Rock-in' Rob-in 'cause we're

real-ly gon-na rock to-night.___ A

pret-ty lit-tle ra-ven at the bird band-stand, taught him how to do the bop and

it was grand. They start-ed go-in' stead-y, and bless my soul, he

out-bopped the buz-zard and the o-ri-ole. He

Route 66

Rhythm Of The Rain

Words and Music by
JOHN GUMMOE

Lis-ten to the rhy-thm of the fall-ing rain,— tell-ing me just what a fool I've been. I wish that it would go and let me cry in vain,— and let me be a-lone a-gain.— The Rain, please tell me, now does that seem fair— for her to steal my heart a-way, when she don't care?— I can't love an-oth-er when my heart's some-where— far a-way.

on-ly girl I care a-bout has gone a-way,— look-in' for a brand new start. But lit-tle does she know that when she left that day,— a-long with her she took my heart.— Rain, won't you tell her that I love her so.— Please ask the sun to set her heart a-glow.— Rain in her heart and let the love we knew— start to grow.

D.C. (To 1st Verse) al Fine

Show Me The Way To Go Home

Words and Music by
IRVING KING

Show me the way to go home, I'm tired and I want to go to bed. I had a lit-tle drink a-bout an hour a-go, and it went right to my head. Wher-ev-er I may roam, on land, or sea, or foam; you will al-ways hear me sing-ing this song: show me the way to go home.

San Francisco Bay Blues

Words and Music by
JESSE FULLER

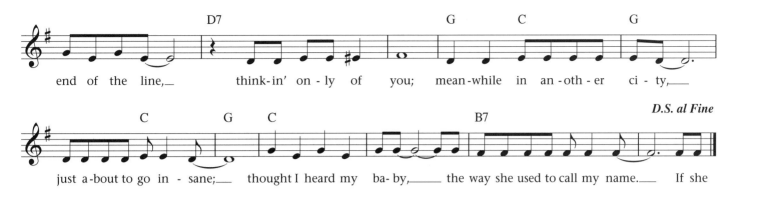

end of the line,___ think-in' on-ly of you; mean-while in an-oth-er ci-ty,___

D.S. al Fine

just a-bout to go in - sane;___ thought I heard my ba-by,____ the way she used to call my name.___ If she

Satin Doll

Words by JOHNNY MERCER
and BILLY STRAYHORN

Music by
DUKE ELLINGTON

Smoothly

Cig - a - rette hold - er, which wigs me, o - ver her shoul - der, she digs me.
Ba - by shall we___ go out skip - pin'? Care - ful a - mi - go, you're flip - pin'.

Out cat - tin' that Sat - in Doll.___ ___ She's
Speaks Lat - in that Sat - in Doll.___

no - bod - y's fool, so I'm play - ing it cool as can be.___ I'll

give it a whirl,__ but I ain't for no girl___ catch - ing me.___

___ *Switch - e - roo - ney.* Tel - e - phone num - bers, well, you know, do - ing my rhum - bas

with u - no, and that 'n' my Sat - in Doll.___

Scarborough Fair/Canticle

Arrangement and Original Counter Melody by
PAUL SIMON and ARTHUR GARFUNKEL

Scotch And Soda

Words and Music by
DAVE GUARD

Sealed With A Kiss

Words by
PETER UDELL

Music by
GARY GELD

Secret Agent Man

Seattle

Words and Music by ERNIE SHELDON,
JACK KELLER and
HUGO MONTENEGRO

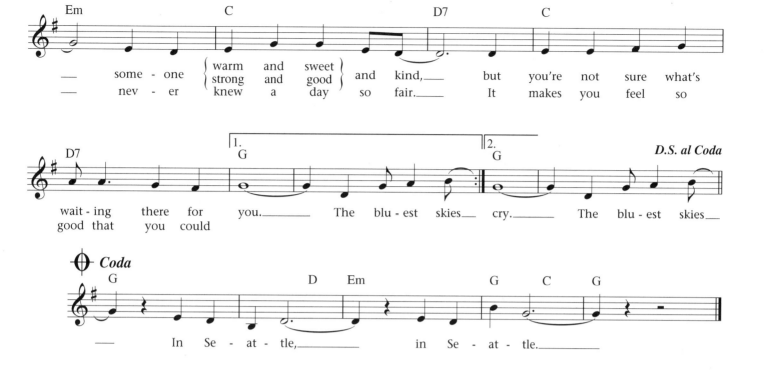

Em   C   D7   C

—   some - one { warm and sweet / strong and good } and kind,___ but you're not sure what's
—   nev - er   knew a day   so fair.___ It makes you feel so

D7   1. G   2. G   *D.S. al Coda*

wait - ing there for you.___ The blu - est skies___ cry.___ The blu - est skies___
good that you could

Coda

G   D Em   G C G

—   In Se - at - tle,___ in Se - at - tle.___

Sherry

Words and Music by
BOB GAUDIO

Snowbird

Words and Music by
GENE MacLELLAN

The Shoop Shoop Song
(It's In His Kiss)

Words and Music by
RUDY CLARK

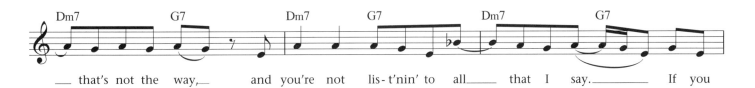

that's not the way,___ and you're not lis- t'nin' to all___ that I say.___ If you

D.S. al Coda
(take 2nd ending)

To Coda ⊕

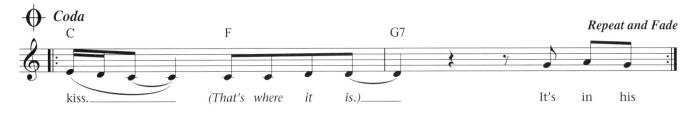

wan - na know___ if he loves you so,___ it's in his kiss.___

⊕ *Coda*

Repeat and Fade

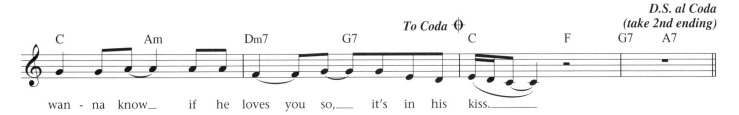

kiss._____ *(That's where it is.)*___ It's in his

305

Singing The Blues

Words and Music by
MELVIN ENDSLEY

1. Well, I nev-er felt more like sing-ing the blues,_ 'cause I nev-er thought_ that
2. nev-er felt more like cry-ing all night,_ 'cause ev-'ry-thing's wrong_ and

I'd ev-er lose_ your love, dear. Why'd you do me this way?_____ Well, I
noth-ing ain't right_ with-out you. You got me sing-ing the blues._____

blues._____ The moon and stars no long-er shine; the dream is gone I thought was mine. There's

noth-ing left for me to do but cry_____ o - ver you._ Well, I

nev-er felt more like run-ning a - way,_____ but why should I go_____ 'cause

I could-n't stay_ with-out you. You got me sing-ing the blues._____

Slow Poke

Words and Music by PEE WEE KING,
CHILTON PRICE and
REDD STEWART

You keep me wait-in' 'til you know it's ag - gra - vat - in'. You're a slow - poke.
Why should I ling - er ev -'ry time you snap your fin - ger, lit - tle slow - poke?

I sit 'n' wor - ry, but you nev - er seem to hur - ry, lit - tle slow - poke.
Why can't you has - ten when you see the time's a - wast - in'? You're a slow - poke,

Time means

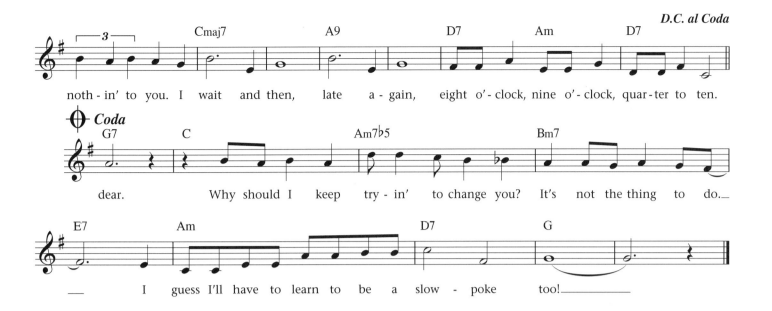

noth-in' to you. I wait and then, late a-gain, eight o'-clock, nine o'-clock, quar-ter to ten.

dear. Why should I keep try-in' to change you? It's not the thing to do.

I guess I'll have to learn to be a slow-poke too!

Soon It's Gonna Rain

Lyrics by
HARVEY SCHMIDT

Music by
TOM JONES

Soon it's gon-na rain, I can see it. Soon it's gon-na rain,
Soon it's gon-na rain, I can feel it. Soon it's gon-na rain;
Then we'll let it rain, we'll not feel it. Then we'll let it rain,

I can tell. Soon it's gon-na rain, what are we gon-na
I can tell. Soon it's gon-na rain, what-'ll we do with
rain pell mell. And we'll not com-plain if it nev-er stops at

do? you? We'll find four limbs of a tree. We'll build four

walls and a floor. We'll bind it o-ver with leaves, then duck in-side to stay.

all. We'll live and love with-in our own four walls.

So Long It's Been Good To Know Yuh
(Dusty Old Dust)

Words and Music by
WOODY GUTHRIE

Additional Lyrics

4. I walked down the street to the grocery store.
It was crowded with people both rich and both poor.
I asked the man how his butter was sold;
he said, "One pound of butter for two pounds of gold."
I said:
Chorus

5. My telephone rang and it jumped off the wall.
That was the preacher a-making a call.
He said, "We're waitin' to tie the knot;
you're gettin' married, believe it or not!"

6. The church it was jammed, the church it was packed;
the pews were so crowded from front to the back.
A thousand friends waited to kiss my new bride,
but I was so anxious I rushed her outside.
Told them:
Chorus

Spooky

Words and Music by J.R. COBB,
BUDDY BUIE, HARRY MIDDLEBROOKS
and MIKE SHAPIRO

1. In the cool of the ev-'ning when ev - 'ry-thing is get-tin' kind of
2. al - ways keep me guess-ing, I nev - er seem to know what you are
3. If you de-cide___ some day to stop this lit-tle game that you are

groo - vy; I call you up and ask you if you'd
think - ing. And if a fel - ler looks at you, it's for
play - ing; I'm gon - na tell you all the things my

like to go with me and see a mo - vie.
sure your lit - tle eye will be a - wink - ing.
heart's___ been a - dy - ing to be say - ing. Ah,

First you say no,___ you've got some plans for to - night,___ and then you
I get con - fused___ 'cause I don't know where I stand,___ and then you
just like a ghost,___ you've been a - haunt - ing my dreams,___ so I'll pro -

stop and say, "All right."
smile and hold my hand.
pose on Hal - low - een.

1., 2.
Love is kind - a craz - y with a
Love is kind - a craz - y with a

spook - y lit - tle girl like you.___ 2. You
spook - y lit - tle girl like you.___

3.
Love is kind - a craz - y with a spook - y lit - tle girl like you. Spook - y.

Repeat and Fade

Somethin' Stupid

Words and Music by
C. CARSON PARKS

Somewhere, My Love

Lyric by
PAUL FRANCIS WEBSTER

Music by
MAURICE JARRE

A Song Of Old Hawaii

Words and Music by GORDON BEECHER
and JOHNNY NOBLE

Dreamily

There's the per - fume of a mil - lion flow - ers cling - ing to the heart of old Ha - wai - 'i. There's a rain - bow trade - wind fol - low - ing the show - ers bring - ing me a part of old Ha - wai - 'i.

sigh - ing in the heav - ens, sing - ing me a song of old Ha - wai - 'i.

Fine

There's a sil - ver moon, a sym - pho - ny of

D.S. al Fine

stars. There's a hu - la tune and the hum of soft gui - tars. There's the

Sophisticated Hula

Words and Music by
SOL BRIGHT

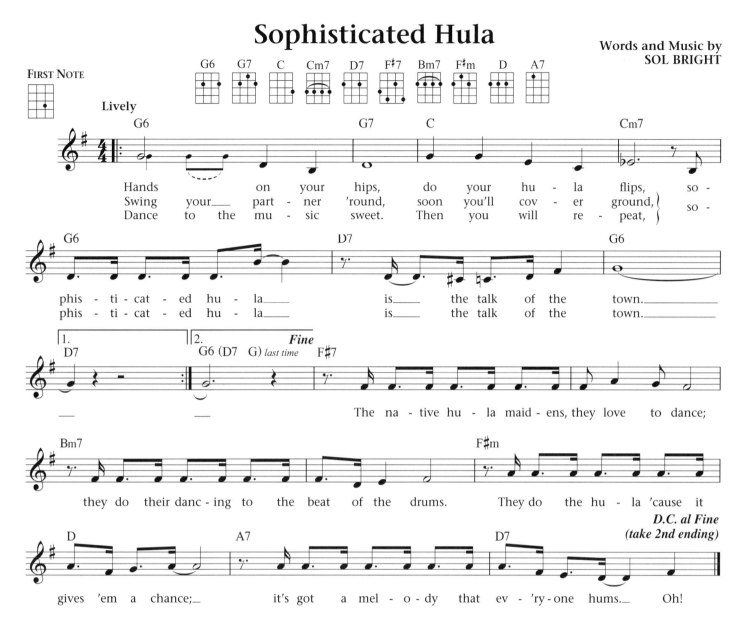

FIRST NOTE

G6 G7 C Cm7 D7 F#7 Bm7 F#m D A7

Lively

G6 **G7** **C** **Cm7**

Hands on your hips, do your hu - la flips, so -
Swing your part - ner 'round, soon you'll cov - er ground, so -
Dance to the mu - sic sweet. Then you will re - peat,

G6 **D7** **G6**

phis - ti - cat - ed hu - la___ is___ the talk of the town.___
phis - ti - cat - ed hu - la___ is___ the talk of the town.___

1. **2.** *Fine*
D7 **G6 (D7 G)** *last time* **F#7**

The na - tive hu - la maid - ens, they love to dance;

Bm7 **F#m**

they do their danc - ing to the beat of the drums. They do the hu - la 'cause it

D **A7** *D.C. al Fine*
(take 2nd ending)
D7

gives 'em a chance;___ it's got a mel - o - dy that ev - 'ry - one hums.___ Oh!

Southern Nights

Words and Music by
ALLEN TOUSSAINT

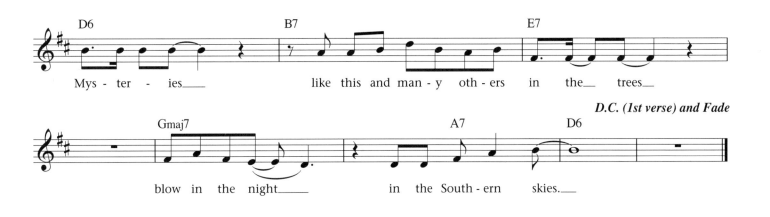

Mys - ter - ies___ like this and man - y oth - ers in the__ trees__

D.C. (1st verse) and Fade

blow in the night___ in the South - ern skies.__

Spanish Eyes

Words by CHARLES SINGLETON
and EDDIE SNYDER

Music by
BERT KAEMPFERT

Blue___ Span - ish eyes,___ tear - drops are fall - ing from your Span - ish
Blue___ Span - ish eyes,___ pret - ti - est eyes in all of Mex - i -

eyes.___ Please,___ please don't cry,___ this is just "a - di -
co.___ True___ Span - ish eyes,___ please smile for me once

os" and not good - bye.___ Soon___ I'll re - turn,___
more be - fore I go.___

bring - ing you all the love your heart can hold.___ Please___ say "Si

si," say you and your Span - ish eyes will wait for me.___

___ say you and your Span - ish eyes will wait for me.___

Stayin' Alive

Words and Music by BARRY GIBB,
ROBIN GIBB and MAURICE GIBB

stay-in' a - live,_ stay-in' a - live._ Ah, ha, ha, ha, stay-in' a - live._____

D　　　　　　　　　Em　　Bm7　　　　　Em7　　　　　　　　　　Em7

Well now, I __

A7

Life go - in' no - where._____ Some - bod - y help me._____

Em7

Some - bod - y help_ me, yeah._____

A7

Life go - in' no - where._____ Some - bod - y help_ me, yeah._____

D.S. 1st Verse and Fade

Em7

Stay - in' a - live._____ Well, you can tell___

Stoney End

Words and Music by
LAURA NYRO

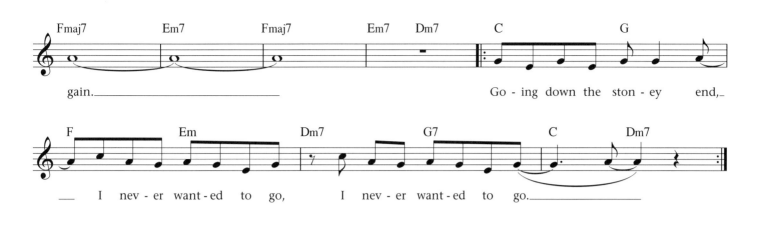

Stormy

Words and Music by
J.R. COBB and BUDDY BUIE

Stop! In The Name Of Love

Words and Music by LAMONT DOZIER,
BRIAN HOLLAND and
EDWARD HOLLAND

Sugar, Sugar

Words and Music by
ANDY KIM and JEFF BARRY

Sukiyaki

English lyrics by
TOM LESLIE and BUZZ CASON

Words and Music by
HACHIDAI NAKAMURA and ROKUSUKE EI

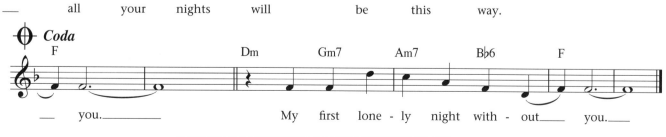

1. I'll hold my head up high_____ look - ing
2. I know the night will hide_____ sad - ness I
3. So I'll go on a - lone,_____ pre - tend - ing

to the sky,_____ so they won't see all the
feel in - side._____ No one will know, for the
you're not gone,_____ but I can't hide all the

tears that are in my eyes._____ No one will know
smile on my lips won't tell them I'm los - ing you
mo - ments of love we knew:_____ Mem - 'ries of you

I'm go - ing through my first lone - ly night with - out_____
and go - ing through my first lone - ly night with - out_____
as I go through my first lone - ly night with - out_____

1. _____ you._____
2. _____ you._____ As I walk a - lone,_____

_____ the lone - ly winds seem to say: From this dark - ness on_____

_____ all your nights will be this way.

D.C. al Coda

Coda

_____ you._____ My first lone - ly night with - out_____ you._____

Summer Breeze

Words by
JAMES SEALS

Music by JAMES SEALS
and DASH CROFTS

See the cur - tains hang - in' in the win - dow
See the pa - per lay - in' on the side - walk,
See the smile a - wait - in' in the kitch - en,

___ in the eve - ning on a Fri - day night.
___ a lit - tle mu - sic from the house next door.
___ food cook - in' and the plates for two.

A lit - tle light a - shin - in' through the win - dow
So I walk on up to the door - step,
Feel the arms that reach___ out to hold___ me,

___ lets me know ev - 'ry - thing's all right.
___ through the screen and a - cross the floor.
___ in the eve - ning when the day is through.

Sum - mer breeze___ makes me feel fine,___ blow - in' through the jas - mine in my

mind.___ Sum - mer breeze___ makes me feel fine,___

blow - in' through the jas - mine in my mind.

Sweet days of sum - mer the jas - mine's in bloom,___ Ju - ly is dressed___ up and

Summer Wind

English Words by JOHNNY MERCER
Original German Lyrics by HANS BRADTKE

Music by
HENRY MAYER

Summer In The City

Words and Music by
JOHN SEBASTIAN, STEVE BOONE
and MARK SEBASTIAN

Last time fade out

A Sunday Kind Of Love

Words and Music by LOUIS PRIMA,
ANITA NYE LEONARD, STANLEY RHODES
and BARBARA BELLE

Sunshine
(Go Away Today)

Words and Music by
JONATHAN EDWARDS

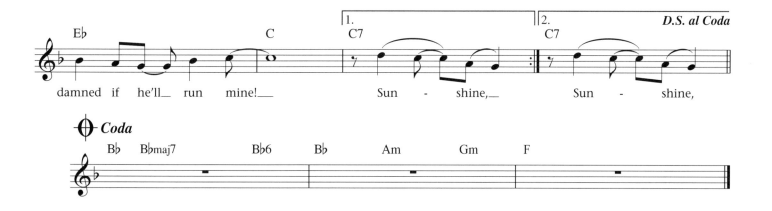

damned if he'll_ run mine!_   Sun - shine,_   Sun - shine,

Summertime

Music and Lyrics by GEORGE GERSHWIN,
DU BOSE and DOROTHY HEYWARD
and IRA GERSHWIN

Sum - mer - time___ and the liv - in' is eas - y._ Fish are

jump - in',_ and the cot - ton is high._ Your dad - dy's rich,_

and your ma is good - look - in'._ So hush, lit - tle ba - by, don't_ you

cry. One of these morn - in's, you're goin' to rise_ up sing - in'._

_ Then you'll spread your wings_ and you'll take to the sky._

_ But 'til that morn - in'_ there's a - noth - in' can harm you_

with Dad - dy and Mam - my stand - ing by._

Sunshine Superman

Words and Music by
DONOVAN LEITCH

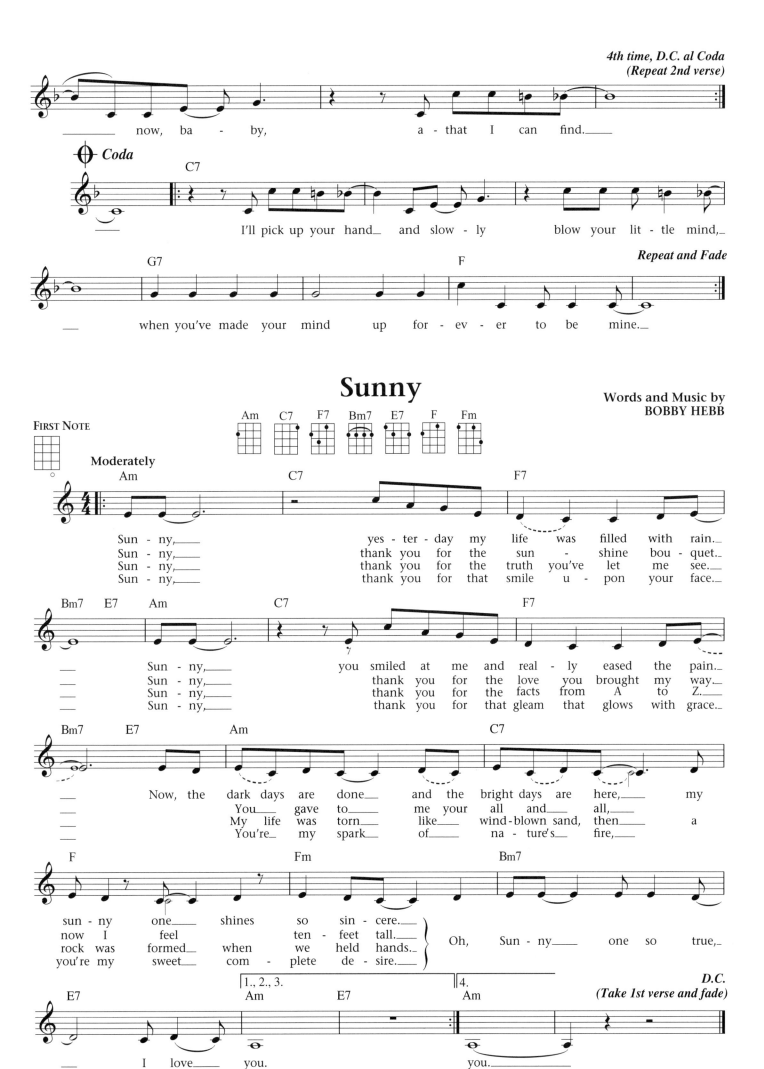

Sunny

Words and Music by
BOBBY HEBB

Sweet Caroline

Words and Music by
NEIL DIAMOND

Sweet Someone

Words by
GEORGE WAGGNER

Music by
BARON KEYES

Sweet Georgia Brown

Words and Music by BEN BERNIE,
MACEO PINKARD and KENNETH CASEY

No gal made__ has got a shade__ on sweet Geor gia Brown.__

Two left feet,__ but oh, so neat,__ has sweet Geor-gia Brown.__

They all sigh__ and wan-na die__ for sweet Geor-gia Brown.__ I'll tell__ you just

why,__ you know__ I don't lie, not much!

It's been said__ she
All those tips__ the

knocks 'em dead,__ when she lands in town.__ Since she came,__ why
por-ter slips__ to sweet Geor-gia Brown;__ they buy clothes__ at

it's a shame__ how she cools 'em down.__ Fel - lers__
fash-ion shows__ with one dol-lar down.__ Oh, boy,__

she can't get__ are fel-lers__ she ain't met.__ Geor-gia claimed__ her,
tip your hats,__ oh, joy,__ she's the "cat's."__ Who's that, mis - ter?

1. F   A7
2. F

Geor-gia named__ her, sweet Geor-gia Brown.__
'Tain't her sis - ter, sweet Geor-gia Brown.__

Sweet Pea

Words and Music by
TOMMY ROE

Sway
(Quien Sera)

English Words by
NORMAN GIMBEL

Spanish Words and Music by
PABLO BELTRAN RUIZ

Tammy

Words and Music by
JAY LIVINGSTON and RAY EVANS

Take A Chance On Me

Words and Music by
BENNY ANDERSSON and
BJÖRN ULVAEUS

339

Take Me Home, Country Roads

Words and Music by JOHN DENVER,
BILL DANOFF and TAFFY NIVERT

should have been home yes-ter-day,___ yes-ter-day.___ Coun-try

roads,___ take__ me home,___ coun-try roads,___

take__ me home,___ coun-try roads.___

Tears On My Pillow

Words and Music by
SYLVESTER BRADFORD and AL LEWIS

FIRST NOTE

Moderately

1. You don't re-mem-ber me,___ but I re-mem-ber you.___
2. If we could start a new,___ I would-n't hes-i-tate,___
3. Be-fore you go a-way,___ my dar-ling think of me.___

'Twas not so long a-go,___ you broke my heart in two.___
I'd glad-ly take you back___ and tempt the hand of fate.___ } Tears__ on my pil-low,___
There may still be a chance___ to end my mis-er-y.___

1.
pain___ in my heart___ caused___ by you.___

2., 3.
pain,___ in my heart__ caused__ by

Fine
you___ hoo-hoo-hoo-hoo - hoo. Love is not a gad-get,___ love is not a toy.

D.C. al Fine
(take 2nd ending)

When you find the one you love, she'll fill your heart___ with joy.

Tea For Two

Words by
IRVING CAESAR

Music by
VINCENT YOUMANS

Moderato

Pic - ture you up - on my knee, just tea for two and two for tea; just
Day will break and you'll a - wake and start to bake a sug - ar cake just for

To Coda

me for you and you for me a - lone._____ No - bod - y near us to
me to take for all the boys to

see us or hear us; no friends or re - la - tions on week - end va - ca - tions. We

D.C. al Coda

won't have it known, dear, that we own a tel - e - phone, dear.

Coda

see._____ We will raise a fam - i - ly, a boy for you, a

girl for me. Oh, can't you see how hap - py we would be?_____

Teach Your Children

Words and Music by
GRAHAM NASH

1. You who are on the road must have a code that you can
2. you, of ten-der years, can't know the fears that your el-ders

live by. And so be-come your-self, be-cause the past
grew by. And so, please help them with your youth, they seek the truth

is just a good-bye. Teach your chil-dren well, their fa-ther's
be-fore they can die. Teach your par-ents well, their child-ren's

hell did slow-ly go by. And feed them on your dreams,
hell will slow-ly go by.

the one they pick's the one you'll know by. Don't you

ev-er ask them why, if they told you, you would cry, so just look at them and

Fine   *D.C. al Fine*

sigh. and know they love you. 2. And

A Teenager In Love

Words by
DOC POMUS

Music by
MORT SHUMAN

Tell It Like It Is

Words and Music by GEORGE DAVIS and LEE DIAMOND

Copyright © 1966 (Renewed), 1980 Conrad Music (BMI) and Olrap Publishing (BMI)
All Rights Administered by BMG Rights Management (US) LLC

Tennessee Waltz

Words and Music by
REDD STEWART and
PEE WEE KING

These Foolish Things
(Remind Me Of You)

Words by
HOLT MARVELL

Music by
JACK STRACHEY

1. A cig - a - rette that bears a lip - stick's trac - es,
2. The winds of March that make my heart a danc - er;
3. The smile of Turn - er and the scent of ros - es,

an air - line tick - et to ro - man - tic plac - es,
a tel - e - phone that rings but who's to an - swer?
the wait - ers whist - ling as the last bar clos - es,

and still my heart has wings:_
Oh, how the ghost of you
the song that Cros - by

These fool - ish things re - mind me of you.
A tin - kling pia - no in the

next a - part - ment, those stum - bling words that told you what my heart meant,

a fair - ground's paint - ed swings:_ these fool - ish things re - mind me of

you. You came, you saw, you con - quer'd me.

When you did that to me, I knew some - how this had to be.

These fool - ish things re - mind me of you.

2. clings.
3. sings.

That's The Way
(I Like It)

Words and Music by
HARRY WAYNE CASEY
and RICHARD FINCH

Till There Was You

Words and Music by
MEREDITH WILLSON

Time After Time

Words by
SAMMY CAHN

Music by
JULE STYNE

350

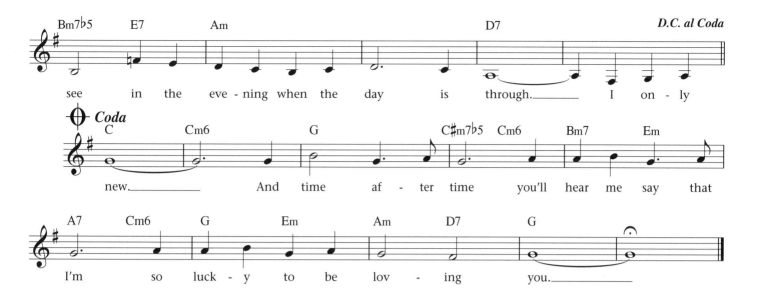

There'll Be Some Changes Made

Words by
BILLY HIGGINS

Music by
W. BENTON OVERSTREET

They Call The Wind Maria

Words by
ALAN JAY LERNER

Music by
and FREDERICK LOEWE

This Is My Song

Words and Music by
CHARLES CHAPLIN

This Magic Moment

Words and Music by DOC POMUS
and MORT SHUMAN

Tip-Toe Thru' The Tulips With Me

Words by
AL DUBIN

Music by
JOE BURKE

Tip - toe to the win - dow, by the win - dow, that is
Tip - toe from your pil - low to the shad - ow, of a
kiss you in the gar - den, in the moon - light, will you

where I'll be. Come
wil - low tree. And } tip - toe thru' the tu - lips with me.____
par - don me? Come }

1.
____ ____

2., 3. *Fine*
Knee deep____ in flow - ers we'll stray;____

____ we'll keep____ the show - ers a - way.____ And if I

Thriller

Words and Music by
ROD TEMPERTON

no one's gon-na save__ you from the beast__ a-bout to strike.__ You know, it's
ain't no sec-ond chance__ a-gainst the thing__ with for-ty eyes.__ You know, it's
I could thrill you more__ than an-y ghost__ would dare to try.__ Girl, this is

thrill-er,__ thrill-er night. You're fight-ing for your life__ in-side a
thrill-er,__ thrill-er night. You're fight-ing for your life__ in-side a
thrill-er,__ thrill-er night, so let me hold you tight__ and share a

To Coda ⊕

1.
kill-er thrill-er to-night.__

2.
kill-er thrill-er to-night. Night crea-tures call and__ the

dead start to walk in their mas-quer-ade There's__

__ no__ es-cap-in'__ the jaws of__ the a-lien__ this time._____
(They're o-pen

This is__ the end of your life._____
wide.)

D.C. al Coda

⊕ **Coda** **Repeat ad lib.**

kill-er thrill-er.

See additional lyrics

Additional Lyrics (Spoken)

4. Darkness falls across the land.
   The midnight hour is close at hand.
   Creatures crawl in search of blood
   to terrorize y'awl's neighborhood.
   And whosoever shall be found
   without the soul for getting down,
   must stand and face the hounds of hell
   and rot inside a corpse's shell.

5. The foulest stench is in the air,
   the funk of forty thousand years.
   And grizzly ghouls from every tomb
   are closing in to seal your doom.
   And though you fight to stay alive,
   your body starts to shiver.
   For no mere mortal can resist
   the evil of the thriller. *(Demonic laughter)*

Time After Time

Word and Music by CYNDI LAUPER and ROB HYMAN

To Love Somebody

Words and Music by
BARRY GIBB and ROBIN GIBB

To Sir, With Love

Words by
DON BLACK

Music by
MARC LONDON

© 1967 (Renewed 1995) SCREEN GEMS-EMI MUSIC INC.

361

Tomorrow

Lyric by
MARTIN CHARNIN

Music by
CHARLES STROUSE

Traces

Words and Music by
J.R. COBB and BUDDY BUIE

Top Of The World

Words and Music by JOHN BETTIS
and RICHARD CARPENTER

Too Young

Words by
SYLVIA DEE

Music by
SID LIPPMAN

Tracy

Words and Music by
PAUL VANCE and
LEE POCKRISS

* You can substitute E7 if necessary.

Travelin' Man

Words and Music by
JERRY FULLER

Twilight Time

Lyric by
BUCK RAM

Music by MORTY NEVINS
and AL NEVINS

Undecided

Words by
SID ROBIN

Music by
CHARLES SHAVERS

A Ukulele And You

Words and Music by
JIM BELOFF

FIRST NOTE

Moderately

Am
Boy I love a big band, 'spe-cially when it swings; or-ches-tras are thrill-ing,
Man I love a man-sion, sit-ting on a hill, serv-ants by the doz-ens,

Dm

E7
love to hear those strings. Love to sing for thou-sands in a con-cert hall, but
bend-ing to my will, and a grand pi-a-no, 'neath a chan-de-lier. But

F7 **Am** **E7**
late-ly I've been think-ing, what's the harm in thin-king small... Give me a
late-ly I've been think-ing, what is mu-sic to my ear... is just a

C **D7**
u-ku-le-le__ and you, a u-ku-le-le__ and you. Just

G7 **C**
give me a uke, and a song_ to sing,_ and you to sing it to.____ Give me a

C **D7**
u-ku-le-le__ and you, no big hul-la-ba-loo. When

G7 *To Coda* ⊕ **C**
push comes to shove, you know what I love?_ A u-ku-le-le and you.

F **Am**
Gee, I love a par-ty, mix-ing with the stars, la-dies in their dia-monds,_

men with their ci - gars.   All the pret - ty peo - ple   al - ways hav - ing fun,   but

G7   *D.S. al Coda*

late - ly I've been think -ing,___ af - ter all is said and done...___   give me a

Coda   *G7*   *C*

u - ku - le - le,___ an oo - koo - le - le,___ a u - ku - le - le___ and you_____

Up Around The Bend

Words and Music by
JOHN FOGERTY

FIRST NOTE

D   A   G

Moderately
D   *A*

1. There's a place___ up a -head and I'm go - in'   just as fast___ as my
2. Bring a smile___ and a song for the ban - jo,   bet - ter get___ while the
3. You can pon - der per - pet - u - al mo - tion,   fix your mind___ on a
4. Catch a ride___ to the end of the high - way   and we'll meet___ by the

D

feet can fly.___   Come a - way,___ come a - way if you're go - in',
get - tin's good.___   Hitch a ride___ to the end of the high - way
crys - tal day.___   Al - ways time___ for a good con - ver - sa - tion,
big red tree.___   There's a place___ up a -head and I'm go - in';

A   *D*   *G*   *D*

leave the sink - in' ship be - hind.___   )
where the ne - ons turn to wood.___   )   Come on the ris - in'
there's an ear___ for what you say.___   )
come a - long, come a - long with me.___   )

| 1., 2., 3. | | | 4. | | |

A   *G*   *D*   *A*   *A*   *D*

wind,   we're go - in' up a - round the bend.   bend.

Ukulele Central

Words by
CHRIS LESLIE

Music by
RIC SANDERS

First Note

With a swing feel

Repeat 4 times

1. Land- ing in eigh- teen- sev- en- ty- nine___ at Hon- o-
lu- lu___ in a bag,___ the twen- ty- third of Au- gust,___ on a
ship called the Ra- vens- crag,___ Fer- nan- dez,___ he was grate- ful___ to make___
___ dry land___ a- gain.___ So he played on a lit- tle gui- tar___
___ he'd brought___ from Spain.___ 2. It caught on with the lo- cal boys___ on
white sands by the sea;___ beau- ti- ful Ha- wai- ian mel- o- dies,___ pluck- ing
G, C, A, and E.___ Some were built by Man- u- el Nu- nes,___ and Au-
gust- o Di- as as well.___ At a store in Hon- o- lu- lu___ they'd just sell.

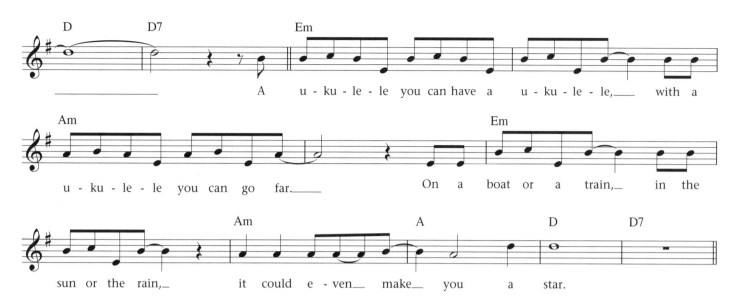

A u - ku - le - le you can have a u - ku - le - le,____ with a

u - ku - le - le you can go far.____ On a boat or a train,__ in the

sun or the rain,__ it could e - ven__ make__ you a star.

Additional Lyrics

3. The Panama Canal was finished,
San Fransisco held a ball.
The uke came in from Hawaii
and was heard by one and all.
"On The Beach At Waikiki"
was the best-known song of them all.
Everywhere it played, a ukulele craze was born.

4. Tin Pan Alley came on the scene,
writing novelty songs.
Everybody started buying ukes
joining in and strumming along.
On a Regal or a Martin,
Harmony or TV Pal.
Even played by Betty Grable –
Oh what a gal!
Chorus

5. The voice of Jiminy Cricket
was a ukulele player so fine.
Konter flew one to the North Pole,
Lyle Ritz played jazz for a time.
George Formby a Wigan Hero;
Tiny Tim was singing so high.
Now the Ukulele "O" of G.B.
spreads its fame far and wide. *(Intrumental)*

6. George and Paul and Joe Brown,
Viv Stanshall, Lucile Ball.
Blue Hawaiian Elvis,
Roy Smeck and Wendell Hall.
Leslie Sarony and Arthur Godfrey could be seen.
Not forgetting the Ukulele Lady Queen –
May Singhi Breen.

7. So what are you waiting for?
It's better than riches and wealth.
Strumming just takes those blues away,
it should be part of the National Health.
Take time to tune and to ponder,
may a song make your day just a breeze.
Take a uke in hand,
may all your dogs have fleas!
Chorus (2 times)

Walk Away Renee

Words and Music by MIKE BROWN,
TONY SANSONE and BOB CALILLI

1. And when I see the sign that points one way;
2. From deep in-side the tears that I forced to cry,
3. Your name and mine in-side a heart up-on a wall

the lot we used to pass by ev-'ry day.
from deep in-side the pain that I chose to hide.
still finds a way to haunt me, though they're so small.

Just walk a-way Re-nee, you won't see me fol-low you

back home.

1., 3. The emp-ty side-walks on my block are not the same,
2. Now as the rain beats down up-on my wear-y heart,

1., 3.   Fine   2.

you're not to blame.
for me it cries.

Just walk a-way, Re-nee, you won't see me fol-low you

back home. Now as the rain beats down up-on

D.C. al Fine

my wear-y heart for me it cries.

The Wanderer

Words and Music by
ERNEST MARESCA

Waterloo

Words and Music by BENNY ANDERSSON,
BJÖRN ULVAEUS and STIG ANDERSON

Wa - ter-loo, know - ing my fate___ is to be___

___ with you, Wa -___ Wa - Wa - Wa - Wa - ter - loo, fi -

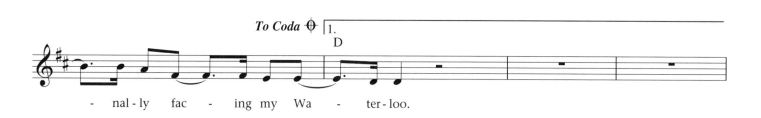

To Coda ⊕ |1.

- nal - ly fac - ing my Wa - ter - loo.

|2. My, my,___ - ter - loo. So how___ could I ev - er re - fuse;___

D.S. al Coda

I feel___ like I win___ when I lose.___ Wa -

⊕ *Coda*

- ter - loo. Whoa___ Wa - ter - loo, know -

- ing my fate___ is to be___ with you, Wa -___ Wa - Wa - Wa - Wa-

- ter - loo, fi - nal - ly fac - ing my Wa - ter - loo.

The Way You Do The Things You Do

Words and Music by
WILLIAM "SMOKEY" ROBINSON
and ROBERT ROGERS

Wedding Bell Blues

Words and Music by LAURA NYRO

We Are The World

Words and Music by LIONEL RICHIE
and MICHAEL JACKSON

What A Diff'rence A Day Made

English Words by
STANLEY ADAMS

Music and Spanish Words by
MARIA GREVER

What Have They Done To My Song, Ma?

Words and Music by
MELANIE SAFKA

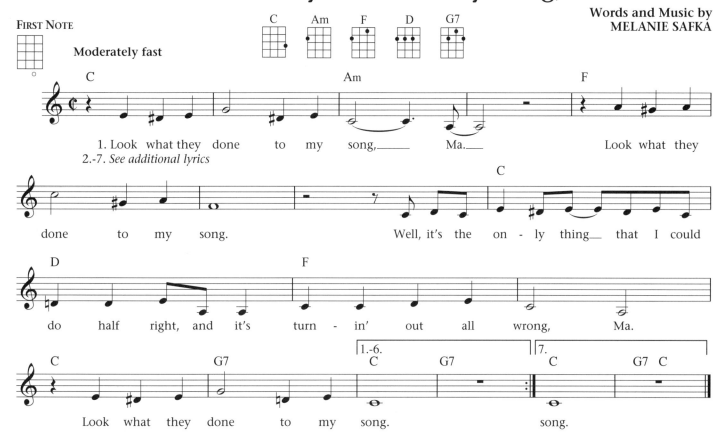

1. Look what they done to my song, Ma. Look what they done to my song. Well, it's the only thing that I could do half right, and it's turnin' out all wrong, Ma. Look what they done to my song.

2.-7. See additional lyrics

Additional Lyrics

2. Look what they done to my brain, Ma.
   Look what they done to my brain.
   Well, they picked it like a chicken bone,
   and I think I'm half insane, Ma.
   Look what they done to my song.

3. I wish I could find a good book to live in.
   Wish I could find a good book.
   Well, if I could find a real good book
   I'd never have to come out and look
   at what they done to my song.

4. But maybe it'll all be alright, Ma.
   Maybe it'll all be o.k.
   Well, if the people are buying tears,
   I'll be rich some day, Ma.
   Look what they done to my song.

5. *Ils ont changé ma chanson Ma.*
   Ils ont changé ma chanson.
   C'est la seule chose que je peux faire
   et ce n'est pas bon Ma.
   Ils ont changé ma chanson.

6. Look what they done to my song, Ma.
   Look what they done to my song.
   Well, they tied it up in a plastic bag
   and turned it upside down, Ma.
   Look what they done to my song.

7. Look what they done to my song, Ma.
   Look what they done to my song.
   It's the only thing I could do alright
   and they turned it upside down.
   Look what they done to my song.

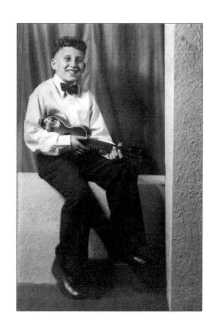

What The World Needs Now Is Love

Lyric by
HAL DAVID

Music by
BURT BACHARACH

When Will I Be Loved

Words and Music by
PHIL EVERLY

Where Have All The Flowers Gone?

Words and Music by
PETE SEEGER

Additional Lyrics

3. Where have all the young men gone, long time passing,
   where have all the young men gone, long time ago?
   Where have all the young men gone, they are all in uniform.
   When will they ever learn, when will they ever learn?

4. Where have all the soldiers gone, long time passing,
   where have all the soldiers gone, long time ago?
   Where have all the soldiers gone, gone to graveyards everyone.
   When will they ever learn, when will they ever learn?

5. Where have all the graveyards gone, long time passing,
   where have all the graveyards gone, long time ago?
   Where have all the graveyards gone, covered with flowers every one.
   When will they ever learn, when will they ever learn?

White Sandy Beach

Words and Music by
WILLY DANN

Who's Sorry Now

Words by BERT KALMER
and HARRY RUBY

Music by
TED SNYDER

Who's sor-ry now? Who's sor-ry now? Whose heart is ach-ing for break-ing each vow? Who's sad and blue? Who's cry-ing too? Just like I cried o-ver you._____ Right to the end, just like a friend, I tried to warn you some-how._____ You had your way, now you must pay; I'm glad that you're sor-ry now._____

Wanderin'

American

1., 5. My dad-dy is an en-gi-neer,_____ my broth-er drives a hack. My
2. I've been a-wan-der-in'____ ear-ly and_____ late, from
3. work-in' in the ar-my,_____ work-in' on a farm; and
4. snakes in the o-cean,_____ eels in the sea, and

sis-ter takes in wash-ing,_____ and the ba-by balls the jack;
New York Cit-y_____ to the Gold-en Gate;
all I've got to show is the mus-cle in my arm;
a red-head-ed wom-an_____ made a wreck of me;

And it

looks like___ I'm nev - er gon - na cease___ my wan - der - in'.

2. Oh,
3. Been
4. There's
5. My

Will You Love Me Tomorrow
(Will You Still Love Me Tomorrow)

Words and Music by
GERRY GOFFIN and
CAROLE KING

1. To - night you're mine___ com - plete - ly,
2. Is this a last - ing treas - ure,
3. I'd like to know___ that your___ love

you give your love___ so sweet - ly,
or just a mo - ment's pleas - ure?
is love I can___ be sure___ of.

To - night the light___
Can I be - lieve___
So tell me now___

of love is in your eyes. }
the mag - ic of your sigh? }
and I won't ask a - gain. }

Will you still love me to -

mor - row? row? row? To - night with words un - spok - en,

you say that I'm the on - ly one,___ but will my heart be

bro - ken___ when the night___ meets the morn - ing sun?___

Coda

row? Will you still love me to - mor - row?

White Rabbit

Words and Music by
GRACE SLICK

Windy

Words and Music by
RUTHANN FRIEDMAN

Red Queen's off___ with her head, re - mem - ber what the Dor - mouse said,___ "Feed your head.___ Feed your head."___

1., 3. Who's peek - in' out from un - der a stair - way, call - ing a name that's light- - er than air? Who's bend - in' down to give___ me a rain - bow? Ev - 'ry - one knows it's Wind - y.

2. Who's trip - pin' down the streets___ of the cit - y, smil - in' at ev - 'ry - bod- - y she sees? Who's reach - ing out to cap - ture a mo - ment?

And Wind - y has storm - y___ eyes___ that flash___ at the sound of___ lies.___ And Wind - y has wings to___ fly___ a - bove the clouds,___ a - bove the clouds,___ a - bove the clouds,___ a - bove the clouds.___

With A Little Luck

Words and Music by
PAUL McCARTNEY

A Wonderful Day Like Today

Words and Music by
LESLIE BRICUSSE and
ANTHONY NEWLEY

Wonderful! Wonderful!

Words by
BEN RALEIGH

Music by
SHERMAN EDWARDS

Worried Man Blues

Traditional

FIRST NOTE

G C D7

Moderately

G

1. It takes a wor - ried man___ to sing a wor - ried song. It
went a - cross the riv - er, and I lay down to sleep. I
asked that judge, "Tell me,___ what's gon - na be my fine?" I
looked down the road,___ as far as I could see. I

C G

takes a wor - ried man___ to sing a wor - ried song. It
went a - cross the riv - er, and I lay down to sleep. I
asked that judge, "Tell me,___ what's gon - na be my fine?" I
looked down the road,___ as far as I could see. I

takes a wor - ried man___ to sing a wor - ried song. I'm wor - ried
went a - cross the riv - er, and I lay down to sleep. When I woke
asked that judge, "Tell me,___ what's gon - na be my fine?" Twen - ty - one years
looked down the road,___ as far as I could see; a little, bit - ty

D7 G *Fine* *Last time D.S. al Fine*

now, but I won't be wor - ried long._____ 2. I
up, had shack - les on my feet._____ 3. I
on the Rock - y Moun - tain line._____ 4. I
hand was wav - ing af - ter me._____

Y.M.C.A.

**Words and Music by JACQUES MORALI,
HENRI BELOLO and VICTOR WILLIS**

Additional Lyrics

3. Young man, are you listening to me?
   I said, young man, what do you want to be?
   I said, young man, you can make real your dreams,
   but you've got to know this one thing.

4. No man does it all by himself.
   I said, young man, put your pride on the shelf.
   And just go there to the Y.M.C.A.;
   I'm sure they can help you today.
   Chorus

5. Young man, I was once in your shoes.
   I said, I was down and out and with the blues.
   I felt no man cared if I were alive.
   I felt the whole world was so jive.

6. That's when someone came up to me
   and said, "Young man, take a walk up the street.
   It's a place there called the Y.M.C.A.
   They can start you back on your way."
   Chorus

You And I

You Are The Sunshine Of My Life

Words and Music by
STEVIE WONDER

You Belong To Me

Words and Music by PEE WEE KING,
REDD STEWART and CHILTON PRICE

FIRST NOTE

Smoothly

1. See the pyr-a-mids a-long the Nile, watch the sun rise on a
2. See the mar-ket-place in old Al-giers, send the pho-to-graphs and
3. Fly the o-cean in a sil-ver plane, see the jun-gle when it's

To Coda ⊕ | 1.

trop-ic isle, just re-mem-ber, dar-ling, all the while, you be-long to
sou-ve-nirs, just re-mem-ber when a dream ap-pears,
wet with rain. Just re-mem-ber, 'til you're home a-gain,

| 2.

me. you be-long to me. I'll be so a-lone with-

D.C. al Coda

out you. May-be you'll be lone-some, too, and blue.

⊕ **Coda**

you be-long to me.

You Can't Hurry Love

Words and Music by EDWARD HOLLAND,
LAMONT DOZIER and BRIAN HOLLAND

al - most gone, I re - mem - ber Ma - ma said,
hang - ing on; I re - mem - ber Ma - ma said, "Can't hur - ry love,____ no you
"Can't hur - ry love,____ no, you

just have to wait." She said, "Love don't come ea - y,____
just have to wait." She said, "Trust,_____ give____ it time, no

1.
it's a game of give and take.__ You

2.
mat - ter how long it takes."__

No love, love,_____ don't come eas - y, but I

keep on wait - ing, an - ti - ci - pat - ing for that soft voice to talk to

me at night,__ for some ten - der arms_____ to hold__ me tight.__ I keep

wait - ing; you got - ta give and take,__ but it ain't eas - y,____ it ain't

eas - y when Ma - ma said, "You can't hur - ry love.__ no, you just have to wait." She said,

Repeat and Fade

"Love don't come eas - y,_____ it's a game of give and take." You
Trust,_____ give it time, no mat - ter how long it takes." You

401

You Didn't Have To Be So Nice

Words and Music by
JOHN SEBASTIAN
and STEVE BOONE

You Don't Know Me

Words and Music by CINDY WALKER
and EDDY ARNOLD

403

You Got It

Words and Music by ROY ORBISON,
JEFF LYNNE and TOM PETTY

An - y - thing you want, _____ you got it. An - y - thing you need, __

__ you got it. An - y - thing at all. _____

F   A7   Dm   B♭   F   A7

Doo doo doo, doo,   doo.___   Doo doo doo doo,

Dm   B♭   F   A7   Dm   B♭

doo.___   Doo doo doo doo,   you got it.

F   C7   F   Dm

                    I'm glad,___ to give_____ my love

Am   C   F

__   to you.___   I   know__   you

Dm   Am   C7   *D.S. al Coda*

                                                    3

feel_____ the way___   I____ do.___

 *Coda*

C7   F

An - y - thing at all,___ you got it, ba - by._____ you got it!

405

You Won't See Me

Words and Music by
JOHN LENNON and
PAUL McCARTNEY

You're Sixteen
(You're Beautiful And You're Mine)

Words and Music by
RICHARD M. SHERMAN
and ROBERT B. SHERMAN

Young At Heart

Words by
CAROLYN LEIGH

Music by
JOHNNY RICHARDS

Your Mama Don't Dance

Words and Music by JIM MESSINA and KENNY LOGGINS

Your ma - ma don't dance and your dad - dy don't rock and roll.___

Your ma - ma don't dance and your dad - dy don't rock and roll.___

When eve - nin' rolls a - round and it's

time to go to town, where do you go to rock and roll? {The {You

old folks say that you got - ta end your day by ten.___

If you're out on a date and you bring it home late, it's a sin.

There just ain't no ex - cus - in', you know you're gon - na lose___ and nev - er win.___

I'll say it a - gain. And it's all be - cause your

Coda 1

C

pull in - to a drive - in and find a place to park, you

hop in - to the back - seat where you know it's nice and dark. You're

just a - bout to move in, you're think - in' it's a breeze,— there's a

N.C.

light in your eye and then a guy— says, "Out of the car, long - hair," ooh - wee,—

D7   C7

— you're com - in' with me, the lo - cal po -

G   N.C.   D.S. al Coda 2

lice. And it's all be - cause your

Coda 2

G

go to rock and roll? Where do you go to rock and

roll? Where do you go to rock and roll?

Your Mother Should Know

Words and Music by JOHN LENNON
and PAUL McCARTNEY

Your Song

Words and Music by ELTON JOHN
and BERNIE TAUPIN

You've Got A Friend

Words and Music by
CAROLE KING

Am   **D7**   **F**   **C**

Now ain't it good to know that you've___ got a friend,_ when

G   **Gmaj7**   **C**   **F7**

peo-ple can be___ so cold.___ They'll hurt___ you, yes, and de - sert___ you, and

Em   **A7**   **Am**   **D7**   *D.S. al Coda*

take your soul___ if you let them. Oh, but don't you let___ them. You just call___

⊕ *Coda*

C   **Am**   **D7**   **G**

___ there,_ yes, I will._____ You've got a friend._____

C   **G**   **C**   *Repeat and Fade*

You've got a friend._____ Ain't it good___ to know you've got a

Thank You

Our biggest thank yous go to Ronny Schiff and Charylu Roberts...we couldn't have done it without you! Pete McDonnell once again provided the delightful illustrations and Brian O'Keefe was a big help with the music proofing. Also, major thanks to Jeff Schroedl, Dan Bauer, David Dinan, Jerry Muccio, David Jahnke, Denis Kavemeier, Trish Dulka, Laurie Hagopian, Larry Morton, Keith Mardak and everyone else at Hal Leonard Corporation for your enormous help in making the *Daily Ukulele* songbooks a reality. Special thanks, as well, to ukulele clubs everywhere who have embraced *The Daily Ukulele* and made it their club songbook!

The worldwide ukulele community contributed hundreds of great song suggestions for this new collection, many of which we included. A big thank you to the following for your suggestions: Aaron Warren, Ben Hart, Bruce Pasarow, Bud Runion, Cali Rose, Carrie Thompson, Chris Arnott, Dan Arnold, Dave Bogart, Dave Hudson, Dave Kapell, Dave Mascall, David Montoya, David Remiger, Dean Coley, Dee Holm, Ed Vigdor, Ed Wojtowicz, Eric Tisdale, Faith Middleton, Gary Moebus, Grant Ryder, Greg Hawkes, Hillel Wasserman, Ian Whitcomb, Jack Bennett, Jack Fuller, James Jacques, Jeanie Hoover, Jim Lenn, Jim Roberts, Joan Levy, Joanne, Joe Wadanoli, John and Evelyn Chandler, John Penhallow, Judy Taylor, Kelly Trafford, Kurt Siegel, Lalya Gaye, Lauren Agnelli, Laverne, Lawrence, Lil Rev, Louis Dumas, Mark Josephs, Matt Karas, Mike Hammerman, Mike Hater, Mike Hopkins, Mitch Chang, Molly Ungar, Mona Harvey, Nikol Price, Paul Landman, Paul Neri, Pete "Uncle Zac" Zaccagnino, Peter Detloff, Phyllis Webb, Rachel Manke, Ralph Kelley, Raven, Richard Batchelder, Rick Davenport, Ron and Jean Brasefield, Ronnie Blair, Rus Schomers, Ryan Taylor, Scott Ferguson, Scott Spiegler, Shep Stern, Sherral Max, Shirley Brown, Shirley Davis, Stan Smith, Stephen Peterson, Stephen Reed, Steve Awakuni, Suzala, TJB, Tim Mann, Tom Noble, Tom Swicegood, Victoria Vox, Warren Bowman, Wayne Martin, Wendy & Greg (The Edukated Fleas), Wiley Selman.

Finally, a thank you to all who helped in one way or another to make this book what it is, especially: Tony Cappa, Andy Andrews, Jamison Smeltz, Geoff Rezek, Jim "Doctor Uke" Rosokoff, Curt Sheller, Fred Sokolow, Peter Thomas, Shirley Orlando, Susan McCormick, Pat Enos, Paul Cundari, Stephanie Rinaldo (Hollywood Sheet Music), Steve Boisen, Mike Upton, Kristen Helmore, Aldrine Guerrero, Aaron Nakamura, Jim D'Ville, Chris Leslie, Ric Sanders, Todd Rundgren, Lynn Robnett, Jim Bollman, Aaron Stang, Steven Strauss, Kathy Sumpter, The Magic Fluke Co. and Marvin and "Mike" Beloff. And you!

Jim & Liz Beloff

Finding a ukulele at the Pasadena Rose Bowl Flea Market in 1992 inspired Liz and Jim Beloff to start Flea Market Music, Inc., publisher of the popular *Jumpin' Jim's* series of ukulele songbooks including *The Daily Ukulele: 365 Songs For Better Living*. This series is sold worldwide and is distributed by the Hal Leonard Corporation. Jim is also the author of *The Ukulele—A Visual History* (1997 Backbeat Books), and has made three how-to-play DVDs for Homespun Tapes: *The Joy of Uke #1 and #2* and *Jumpin' Jim's Ukulele Workshop*. With a background in film and television graphics, Liz designs the covers and art-directs FMM's songbooks, CDs and DVDs. Jim and Liz regularly perform together at ukulele events playing the unique Fluke, Flea and Firefly ukuleles manufactured by The Magic Fluke Co. They truly believe in their company's motto, "Uke Can Change the World." You can reach them through the Flea Market Music web site at **www.fleamarketmusic.com**.

Rick Scanlan Photography